P9-CDM-858

DATE DUE

DEADLY DISEASES AND EPIDEMICS

SYPHILIS

Second Edition

Anthrax, Second Edition

Antibiotic-Resistant
  Bacteria

Avian Flu

Botulisim

Campylobacteriosis

Cervical Cancer

Chicken Pox

Cholera, Second Edition

Dengue Fever and Other
  Hemorrhagic Viruses

Diphtheria

Ebola

Encephalitis

Escherichia coli
  Infections

Gonorrhea

Hantavirus Pulmonary
  Syndrome

Helicobacter pylori

Hepatitis

Herpes

HIV/AIDS

Infectious Diseases of
  the Mouth

Infectious Fungi

Influenza, Second Edition

Legionnaires' Disease

Leprosy

Lung Cancer

Lyme Disease

Mad Cow Disease

Malaria, Second Edition

Meningitis

Mononucleosis, Second
  Edition

Pelvic Inflammatory
  Disease

Plague, Second Edition

Polio, Second Edition

Prostate Cancer

Rabies

Rocky Mountain Spotted
  Fever

Rubella and Rubeola

Salmonella

SARS, Second Edition

Smallpox

Staphylococcus aureus
  Infections

Streptococcus (Group A)

Streptococcus (Group B)

Syphilis, Second Edition

Tetanus

Toxic Shock Syndrome

Trypanosomiasis

Tuberculosis

Tularemia

Typhoid Fever

West Nile Virus, Second
  Edition

Yellow Fever

DEADLY DISEASES AND EPIDEMICS

SYPHILIS

Second Edition

Brian R. Shmaefsky, Ph.D.

CONSULTING EDITOR
Hilary Babcock, M.D., M.P.H.,
Infectious Diseases Division,
Washington University School of Medicine,
Medical Director of Occupational Health (Infectious Diseases),
Barnes-Jewish Hospital and St. Louis Children's Hospital

FOREWORD BY
David L. Heymann
World Health Organization

CHELSEA HOUSE
PUBLISHERS
An imprint of Infobase Publishing

Syphilis, Second Edition

Copyright © 2010 by Infobase Publishing

Chelsea House
An imprint of Infobase Publishing
132 West 31st Street
New York NY 10001

Library of Congress Cataloging-in-Publication Data

Shmaefsky, Brian.
  Syphilis / Brian Shmaefsky ; consulting editor, Hilary Babcock ; foreword by David Heymann. — 2nd ed.
      p. cm. — (Deadly diseases and epidemics)
  Includes index.
  ISBN-13: 978-1-60413-242-7 (hardcover : alk. paper)
  ISBN-10: 1-60413-242-6 (hardcover : alk. paper) 1. Syphilis—Juvenile literature. I. Title.

  RC201.1.S476 2009
  616.95'13—dc22
                                    2009034276

Chelsea House books are available at special discounts when purchased in bulk quantities for businesses, associations, institutions, or sales promotions. Please call our Special Sales Department in New York at (212) 967-8800 or (800) 322-8755.

You can find Chelsea House on the World Wide Web at http://www.chelseahouse.com

Text design by Terry Mallon
Cover design by Keith Trego
Illustrations by Dale Williams

Printed in the United States of America

Bang MSRF 10 9 8 7 6 5 4 3 2 1

This book is printed on acid-free paper.

All links and Web addresses were checked and verified to be correct at the time of publication. Because of the dynamic nature of the Web, some addresses and links may have changed since publication and may no longer be valid.

Table of Contents

Foreword

Communicable diseases kill and cause long-term disability. The microbial agents that cause them are dynamic, changeable, and resilient: They are responsible for more than 14 million deaths each year, mainly in developing countries.

Approximately 46 percent of all deaths in the developing world are due to communicable diseases, and almost 90 percent of these deaths are from AIDS, tuberculosis, malaria, and acute diarrheal and respiratory infections of children. In addition to causing great human suffering, these high-mortality communicable diseases have become major obstacles to economic development. They are a challenge to control either because of the lack of effective vaccines, or because the drugs that are used to treat them are becoming less effective because of antimicrobial drug resistance.

Millions of people, especially those who are poor and living in developing countries, are also at risk from disabling communicable diseases such as polio, leprosy, lymphatic filariasis, and onchocerciasis. In addition to human suffering and permanent disability, these communicable diseases create an economic burden—both on the workforce that handicapped persons are unable to join, and on their families and society, upon which they must often depend for economic support.

Finally, the entire world is at risk of the unexpected communicable diseases, those that are called emerging or re-emerging infections. Infection is often unpredictable because risk factors for transmission are not understood, or because it often results from organisms that cross the species barrier from animals to humans. The cause is often viral, such as Ebola and Marburg hemorrhagic fevers and severe acute respiratory syndrome (SARS). In addition to causing human suffering and death, these infections place health workers at great risk and are costly to economies. Infections such as Bovine Spongiform Encephalopathy (BSE) and the associated new human variant of Creutzfeldt-Jakob Disease (vCJD) in Europe, and avian influenza A (H5N1) in Asia, are reminders of the seriousness of emerging and re-emerging infections. In addition, many of these infections have the potential to cause pandemics, which are a constant threat to our economies and public health security.

Science has given us vaccines and anti-infective drugs that have helped keep infectious diseases under control. Nothing demonstrates the effectiveness of vaccines better than the successful eradication of smallpox, the decrease in polio as the eradication program continues, and the decrease in measles when routine immunization programs are supplemented by mass vaccination campaigns.

Likewise, the effectiveness of anti-infective drugs is clearly demonstrated through prolonged life or better health in those infected with viral diseases such as AIDS, parasitic infections such as malaria, and bacterial infections such as tuberculosis and pneumococcal pneumonia.

But current research and development is not filling the pipeline for new anti-infective drugs as rapidly as resistance is developing, nor is vaccine development providing vaccines for some of the most common and lethal communicable diseases. At the same time, providing people with access to existing anti-infective drugs, vaccines, and goods such as condoms or bed nets—necessary for the control of communicable diseases in many developing countries—remains a great challenge.

Education, experimentation, and the discoveries that grow from them are the tools needed to combat high-mortality infectious diseases, diseases that cause disability, or emerging and re-emerging infectious diseases. At the same time, partnerships between developing and industrialized countries can overcome many of the challenges of access to goods and technologies. This book may inspire its readers to set out on the path of drug and vaccine development, or on the path to discovering better public health technologies by applying our current understanding of the human genome and those of various infectious agents. Readers may likewise be inspired to help ensure wider access to those protective goods and technologies. Such inspiration, with pragmatic action, will keep us on the winning side of the struggle against communicable diseases.

David L. Heymann
Assistant Director General,
Health Security and Environment
Representative of the Director General for Polio Eradication
World Health Organization
Geneva, Switzerland

1

The Disease Called Syphilis

A 13-year-old boy was admitted to a New Delhi, India, hospital with an unusual condition. His parents noticed a hole in the boy's hard palate after he complained of some pain in his upper jaw. The parents told the physician that the hole had slowly gotten larger since its appearance two to three months earlier. They brought him to the hospital when the sore began to cause difficulty with the boy's eating and speech. A variety of blood tests were done; ultimately, the physicians determined that the boy had had syphilis since birth and that his current symptoms were the first indications of the disease. Physicians discovered that two years prior to the child's birth, the mother had been treated for a then-undiagnosed sexually transmitted disease. Luckily, none of his siblings tested positive for syphilis. His condition had been caught early enough to save his life. Each year approximately half a million infants throughout the world are born with syphilis contracted from the mother.[1]

Even today, people suffering from syphilis elicit a different sentiment than those afflicted with influenza, leukemia, or pneumonia. After all, this devastating disease is attributed almost exclusively to sexual activity. In the past and to some extent today, few people are willing to admit to having syphilis because of the negative social stigma attached to it and the lack of public sympathy for the afflicted. These attitudes made it difficult to track syphilis in its early days and tainted the accuracy of its reporting. Dramatic accounts of the disease followed the precedent set by Italian physician Girolamo Fracastoro in his 1530 work, *Syphilis save morgues Gallicus*:

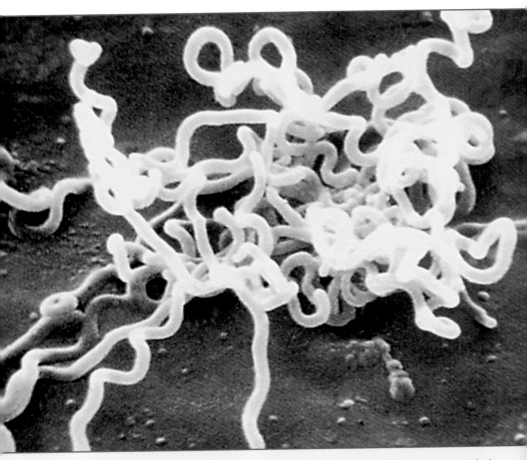

Figure 1.1 *Treponema pallidum*, a spirochete bacterium, has a spiral appearance much like curled spaghetti. *Treponema pallidum* enters the body through mucous membranes, which supply a moist, sticky surface that is attractive to the bacteria. (Centers for Disease Control and Prevention/Dr. David Cox)

He first wore buboes dreadful
To the sight,
First felt strange pains and sleepless
passed the night;
From him the malady received
its name.

The neighboring shepherds caught
the spreading flame:
at last in city and in court
'twas known,
And seized t'ambitious monarch
on his throne.

After Fracastoro, physicians regularly added emotion-filled descriptions to their recording of the disease. This was even true up until the late 1950s in the United States. It was hoped that the horrible imagery surrounding the disease would discourage people from having illicit sex.

Scientists now believe that many of the accounts of syphilis recorded in the 1600s and 1700s were probably not exaggerated. Numerous reports claimed that syphilis produced horrendously painful sores and could quickly lead to mental decay and death. This is rarely noted today. Disease specialists now agree that syphilis appears to have mellowed over time as it spread throughout the human population over the past 500 years. Most of what we know about syphilis today comes from information gathered within the past 100 years of more exacting scientific investigation. Syphilis could not be studied in research animals because it only affects humans. Therefore, everything scientists know about syphilis had to be derived from observation and experimentation on human subjects. Today, syphilis holds few secrets, especially now that the DNA sequence of the disease organism has been completely unveiled.

SYPHILIS: HOW IS IT TRANSMITTED?

Nobody truly knew how syphilis passed from person to person when it first hit Europe around the 1500s. Various ideas were formulated based on the cultural views of disease transmission. Not surprisingly, most people attributed syphilis to sin, consistent with a belief system called spontaneous generation. The idea of spontaneous generation accepted the principle that disease and pests could originate from filth, bad habits, and sinful acts. Through time people realized that it was a sexually transmitted disease. However, it was not until 1905 that they recognized that an infectious **bacterium** caused the disease.

CONDOMS IN EUROPE:
For Syphilis or Birth Control?

Condoms became popular in Europe right around the time syphilis made its nefarious appearance. Some scholars argue that the demand for condoms was prompted by syphilis. Others debate that it was used solely for birth control. A history of the condom and early attitudes about syphilis provide support for both views. The oldest evidence of condom use dates back to ancient Egypt. Drawings from 3,000-year-old Egyptian writings indicate condom use during sex. It is not known if the condom had an unexplained religious significance or was used for birth control. Early Romans also used condoms. However, many believed it was for a ritual that brought strength or providence to the user. Stories recount that the Roman condoms were made from the muscles of defeated enemies.

The first regular use of condoms in Europe started around 1640 in England. Condoms made of cattle, fish, goat, and sheep intestine were discovered in Birmingham, England. The name condom also dates to that time period. It may come from a Dr. Condom who supposedly served King Charles II or a military Colonel Cundum. Some speculate that the English modified the Latin word condo meaning "to store up or hold." It is believed that the condom was prescribed to King Charles to reduce the chances of him fathering illegitimate children from his numerous affairs. Condoms were also distributed to soldiers fighting during the battle between King Charles I and Oliver Cromwell. It may have been recognized then that condoms reduced syphilis transmission from the prostitutes frequented by soldiers. The disease was known to take its toll on soldiers, diminishing their ability to fight in the prolonged battles of that period.

The syphilis bacterium, *Treponema pallidum pallidum,* comes from a long line of harmless bacteria called treponemes that live within the digestive systems of animals ranging from insects to cattle. In order to remain lodged in the body, treponemes possess an attachment structure that permits the bacterium to stick to the lining of the digestive system. The structure ensures that the bacteria are not flushed out of the body. This attachment structure, called a bacterial **ligand**, is a protein found on the surface of the treponeme. The ligand protein attaches to chemicals such as sugars and proteins found throughout an animal's body. Slight alterations of this ligand protein, caused by genetic mutations, change the ability of the ligand to attach to the different parts of an animal. It is believed that changes to this attachment protein permitted the syphilis treponeme to cause the disease in humans. The syphilis treponeme has a form of ligand that enables the organism to bind to a protein called **fibronectin**, which is found in the lining of the body's openings.

Treponemal diseases **bejel** and **yaws** are related to syphilis but more readily transmitted because they require only casual contact with the infected organism. Regular contact is needed to get a full infection. After all, the body does fight off small invasions of bacteria. The transmission of syphilis is more exacting than that of bejel and yaws: Only special regions of the body called **mucous membranes** or mucosal epithelia are susceptible to the syphilis treponeme. One job of these membranes is to protect the body. However, certain organisms can enter the body by exploiting weaknesses in the mucous membrane's defenses. These organisms are able to form openings in the mucous membrane as a means of entering the blood. Once in the blood, the organisms can spread throughout the body.

SYPHILIS: THE DISEASE

Two medical terms have to be defined before continuing with a description of syphilis. The term **sign** describes a medical condition that can be measured or seen, such as redness, a sore, or a swelling. **Symptoms** refer to conditions that cannot be observed and are related to the patient's sensitivity to disease signs. Dizziness, malaise, and pain are all examples of symptoms. Syphilis is a multistage disease with signs and symptoms that resemble those of other diseases. It is often called "the Great Imitator." This explains much of the confusion surrounding syphilis when it was first seen in Europe. Extensive medical studies on humans suffering from syphilis identified five stages of the disease. Stage one is not visible, and it is difficult to predict its onset. The second through fifth stages are clinically visible and are used as the basis of naming the different stages: **primary, secondary, latent**, and **tertiary syphilis**. It is important to remember that syphilis is not a malicious fiend trying to harm those it inhabits. The organism is solely interested in perpetuating its own species. To accomplish this, syphilis treponemes must find food and a safe place in the body of another human. Its metabolic needs can only be satisfied at the expense of the human body. The person invaded by the syphilis treponeme is only a temporary abode. Syphilis must continuously find a way into new hosts to prevent it from dying out with the death of the infected person.

Stage 1: Getting in the Body

Syphilis gets its start in a new person when it is transferred to one of several regions of the body containing mucous membranes. Mucous membranes include the lining or coverings of the digestive system, eyes, reproductive system, and urinary tract. Mucous membranes are loaded with fibronectin and other proteins suitable for microorganism attachment. The syphilis treponeme can stick readily to the eyes, mouth, nasal lining, rectum, urethra, and vagina. Not surprisingly, these are the main locations where syphilis enters the body. A feature of the syphilis treponeme is that it somehow induces

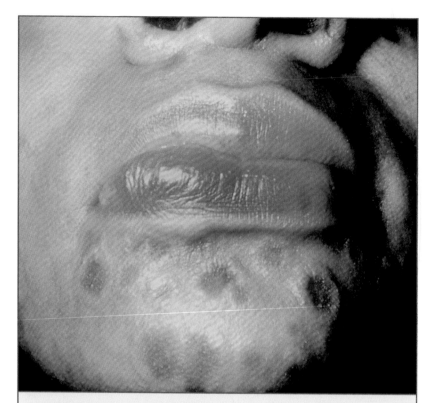

Figure 1.2 Secondary syphilis results in a spotty, copper-colored rash. (Centers for Disease Control and Prevention)

the body to produce a sore or lesion where it attaches to the mucous membrane. Bejel and yaws work in a similar manner except that they attach to skin instead of mucous membranes.

Most cases of syphilis occur when the bacterium is directly transmitted through some form of sexual contact. The organism does not survive well outside of the body. Bacteria related to treponemes have a long association with animals. Most are strictly adapted to the resources provided by the animals they inhabit. The syphilis treponeme can live for six hours outside of the body, and only under favorable conditions such as on moist, warm surfaces protected from light. The syphilis bacterium does not survive long on objects under dry or hot conditions. So, it is unlikely that the disease can spread by objects. However, it is possible that objects freshly contaminated with the syphilis treponeme can infect a person if the object comes in contact with mucous membranes. Syphilis can spread through blood transfusions and contact with open wounds because the organism spends time circulating throughout the body in the blood. Pregnant women can pass syphilis to the fetus through the placenta or during vaginal delivery.

Stage 2: Primary Stage of Syphilis

The syphilis treponeme has now made contact with the body. The organism's next mission is to breach the protective barriers of the body in order for it to gain access to the host's resources. For the syphilis treponeme to survive, it must now find food and a safe refuge to carry out uninterrupted reproduction. The settlement of the syphilis treponeme in the body begins the condition called primary syphilis. This first stage of syphilis usually appears from ten days to about one month after the syphilis treponeme makes contact with the mucous membrane. The infection site forms a small, hard, circular lesion called a **chancre** (pronounced "shanker"). Such lesions usually appear on the penis and in the vagina. However, chancres can also appear on the mouth, nose, rectum, and anus. Chancres start out small and may even be undetectable when they form on a place not so readily visible on the body. At least 70 percent of the people who develop chancres claim that they cause no pain. Other people develop additional problems such as **inflammation** of the lymph nodes near the chancre.

The chancre represents the body's reaction to the syphilis treponeme. This means that the body and not the organism produces the lesion. Unlike many animals, humans naturally produce a strong immune response to spirochetes. The body mounts a full attack involving the cooperation of the white blood cells. The white blood cells produce a variety of chemicals used to fight off the infection. One group of proteins called **antibodies** is designed by the white blood cells to specifically combat foreign substances like the syphilis treponeme. Other antibodies in fact harm the body, creating the lesion where the antibodies are attacking the syphilis treponeme. Unfortunately for the afflicted person, the syphilis treponeme usually grows and spreads faster than the body can destroy it. The chancre is an area of active growth for the syphilis treponeme. Contact with the chancre spreads the disease to another victim. The delicate mucous membranes of the digestive system, reproductive system, and urinary tract are most susceptible to contracting syphilis by contact with a chancre. They are most likely to contact the chancre and are not as good a barrier as skin.

The chancre usually does not last long. For most people it heals after about six weeks, sometimes leaving a scar that can last several months. This leaves people with the misconception that the disease has been fought off by the body and cured. In some treponemal diseases new sores appear, making people realize that the disease is still present. However, in syphilis no new sores arise, giving the appearance that the syphilis treponeme has died off. Actually, just the opposite is true. The syphilis treponeme is now on its way to invading the rest of the body and becoming secondary syphilis.

The form of syphilis that invaded Europe in the 1500s produced a more severe form of chancre. Medical illustrations from the time show that the chancre spread rapidly across the body region that first became infected. The chancres would commonly affect a large region of skin around the reproductive tract opening. Chancres were found just below the chest and above the knees. It was not unusual for the chancres to cover the whole face. Scientists today believe that these extensive sores helped limit the spread of syphilis because it prevented the infected person from having sexual contact.

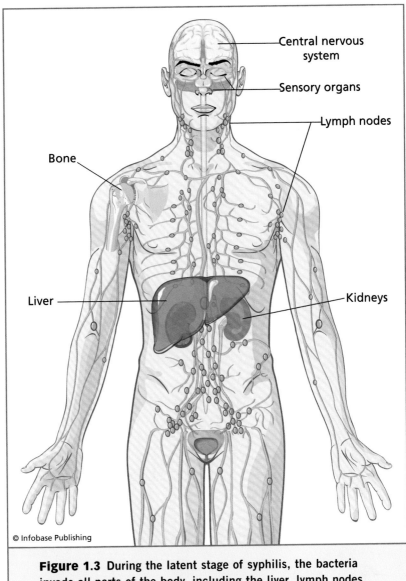

Figure 1.3 During the latent stage of syphilis, the bacteria invade all parts of the body, including the liver, lymph nodes, bones, kidneys, and the nervous system.

Stage 3: Secondary Stage of Syphilis

The syphilis treponeme is now in the body and focused on the goal of reproducing without prematurely killing its host.

Upon healing of the chancre, the syphilis treponeme migrates through the body, starting another series of signs and symptoms called secondary syphilis. These conditions appear two to ten weeks after the chancre hardens and heals. The time it takes for secondary syphilis to appear depends on the age, health, and gender of the person. The disease usually progresses faster and much more severely in people with weakened immune systems. Malnutrition, pre-existing diseases, and stress decrease the immune system's effectiveness, giving the disease more freedom to spread. Ironically, people previously afflicted with bejel and yaws are better able to resist the spread of syphilis at the secondary syphilis stage. Apparently the immune response produced by these syphilis-related diseases protects against syphilis.

Secondary syphilis is difficult to recognize, giving syphilis the label "the Great Imitator." The major signs include a fever, rash, sore throat, and weight loss (see Figure 1.2). In many cases the syphilis treponeme produces sores around the genitals and anus. These sores are highly infectious. Symptoms can consist of headaches, joint pain, and loss of appetite. Unfortunately, many people do not have all of these of these problems. The conditions noted here can also be misinterpreted as many other illnesses ranging from allergies to flu. As all these ailments are appearing, the syphilis treponeme craftily runs down the immune system, making it easier for syphilis to progress in the body and spread to other people. This also makes it easier for other sexually transmitted diseases to attack the body. Secondary syphilis can last from three weeks to as long as a year. Once this stage is completed, it leads into the forth stage of syphilis.

Stage 4: Latent Stage of Syphilis

The latent stage of syphilis was not initially recognized as a distinct period of disease. One reason was that almost half the people getting the disease before treatments were developed died after the disease progressed to secondary syphilis. In addition, at the latent stage all the signs and symptoms of secondary syphilis disappear. Typically, it appears that the

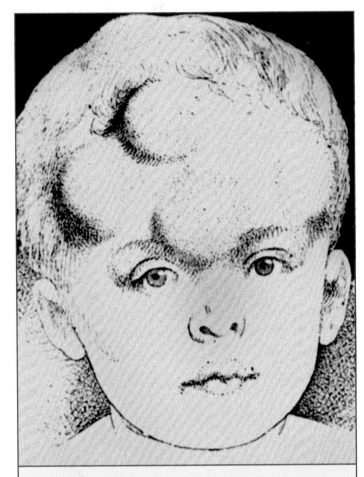

Figure 1.4 Children can acquire syphilis from their mothers who have the disease during pregnancy and/or childbirth. Congenital syphilis can lead to disfigurement of the face, teeth, and internal organs. (National Library of Medicine)

syphilis treponeme has left the body and the person is cured. The latent stage can go on for several months or up to several years. For many people, the syphilis treponeme can remain in the latent stage for the rest of their lives. A lack of signs and symptoms is typical of the latent stage. Some people develop eye maladies and other conditions not directly related to syphilis. Many of these conditions probably arise as a result of a weakened immune system.

During the latent period, *Treponema pallidum pallidum* invades every part of the body (Figure 1.3). The bacteria enter the bones, kidneys, liver, lymph nodes, nervous system, and sensory organs. Bone scarring can occur at this point of the disease. It is not fully understood whether people with latent stage syphilis are able to spread the disease. The syphilis treponeme does not appear in body fluids or sores. There appears, therefore, to be little chance that it can be transmitted to others by contact. However, pregnant women with latent stage syphilis can pass it to the fetus. The organism readily travels across barriers in the placenta to invade the developing baby's body. Children picking up syphilis this way acquire **congenital** syphilis. Congenital syphilis can lead to identifiable disfigurement of the face, internal organs, and teeth (Figure 1.4).

Stage 5: Tertiary Stage of Syphilis

If syphilis leaves the latent stage, it begins an apparently noninfectious but potentially lethal stage called tertiary syphilis. Once again the disease reappears with a host of signs and symptoms. However, this final showing of the disease can lead to rapid death. Tertiary syphilis produces a variety of problems associated with the destruction of major body organs. The most evident but least destructive sign is a skin lesion called **gumma**, or syphiloma, shown in Figure 1.5. Gummas are very painful and can form on internal organs as well. They ultimately cause organ failure and complications leading to death. Bone scarring occurs rapidly during tertiary syphilis, causing the decay of small bones in the face. Damage to the inside of the bones produces a degenerative condition called osteomyelitis. Osteomyelitis, or inflammation of the bone and marrow, is typically caused by bacterial

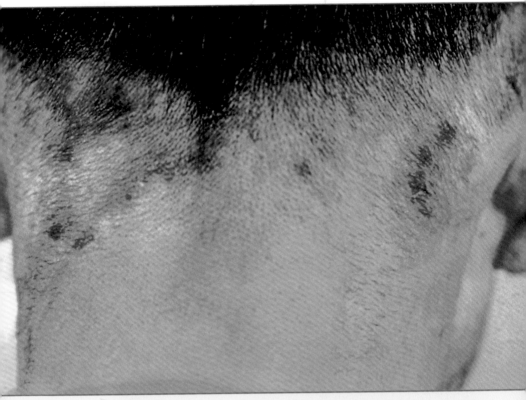

Figure 1.5 The man in this picture has gummas on the back of his neck. Gummas, a symptom of tertiary syphilis, are painful sores that can occur both internally and externally. (Centers for Disease Control and Prevention)

infections. Signs of the condition include fever and sharp pain around the infected bone.

Specific body organs can come under heavy attack by the syphilis treponeme in the tertiary syphilis stage. For example, cardiovascular syphilis is localized to the heart and major blood vessels. This can lead to heart failure or rupture of the major blood vessels. Neurosyphilis results when the syphilis treponeme invades the brain, central nervous system coverings, sensory structures, and major nerves. Personality changes including depression, hallucinations, insanity, mania, and memory loss are typical of this infection. Syphilitic mood changes were blamed for the institutionalization of many famous people accused of having the disease. Paralysis can also occur, as well as the loss of certain senses such as sight, smell, or touch. Some people display seizures and uncontrollable movements similar to muscle spasms. Swelling of the membranes covering the brain creates intense headaches.

Tertiary syphilis can develop three to 15 years after the first signs of a syphilis infection. The age at which a person dies from syphilis depends on the age of infection and the overall health of his or her body. Other STDs, especially AIDS, can greatly increase the chances of dying quickly from damage caused by tertiary syphilis.

People with tertiary syphilis have a reduced chance of spreading the disease through contact. However, open sores on the skin, in the mouth, and in the **reproductive tract** can transmit the organism to the mucous membranes and open wounds of other people. Pregnant women can still pass syphilis to the fetus if they are capable of getting pregnant or carrying out the pregnancy.

In rare instances syphilis was purportedly acquired by handling contaminated body samples and nicking the skin of infected patients during surgery. Scientists are uncertain as to whether the disease can be acquired from dissecting infected cadavers. Cadavers of people with syphilis usually show characteristic damage to the heart and the joints. Lesions in the organs that occur during tertiary syphilis can be confused with body damage caused by other diseases. However, little is know about the persistence of living treponemes in dead bodies. Other diseases, particularly viruses, have been contracted by handling living and dead body specimens.

2

History and Folklore of Syphilis

In his 1530 treatise, Syphilis save marogues Gallicus, *Girolamo Fracastoro gave a description of a new plague that had spread across Europe in the late 1400s. He wrote, "To Naples first it came / from France, and justly took / from France his name / companion from the war. . . ." Fracastoro was poetically describing the disease syphilis, which conjured up such contrasting feelings as bravado and shame. Throughout history, some people commonly used the name "syphilis" to defame others. Others awarded the name as a badge of achievement. History has been of two minds about the disease known today as syphilis. Its role in civilization goes well beyond the disease's true identity and current name.*

Syphilis, like many ancient communicable diseases, was virtually disregarded until detailed accounts of the disease appeared regularly in books on medicine and healing. Earlier stories about syphilis were inconsistent and misleading. This is because syphilis was confused with other diseases. Even some genetic conditions were attributed to the symptoms thought to be caused by syphilis.

Most people today take for granted the fact that communicable diseases are caused by **microbes** such as **bacteria** and **viruses**. Microbes were unknown to the people of the 1400s who first recognized the spread of syphilis. All they knew was that it came about from sensual thoughts or sexual contact. Sin was considered the major cause of the disease.

A NEW DISEASE APPEARS

Many of our ideas about syphilis come from European stories dating back to the time of Christopher Columbus. Syphilis entered Europe

Figure 2.1 Christopher Columbus is one of the earliest historical figures to have an illness documented as syphilis. He was accused of bringing the disease back to Europe from the New World, although historians refute this claim. (Library of Congress)

surrounded by debate and disagreement about its nature and discovery. The first dispute arose from its purported date of discovery. Some argue that syphilis first appeared in Naples, Italy, during the disease outbreak of 1495. Hence, the ignoble disease was coined Neapolitan Disease or *mal de Naples.* Nobody knew how the disease arose; therefore it was assumed that it originated in Naples. Others thought the origin was from an outbreak in nearby Venice and gave it the name Venetian Disease.

These names for syphilis did not make many Italians happy. After all, syphilis was associated with sexual activity that was considered taboo. Therefore many Italians argued that Christopher Columbus's crew brought this plague to Italy from the New World. Italians then felt free to rename the disease the "Spanish Disease," referring to the Spanish crew that served Columbus on his journey. As expected, the Spanish scoffed at this suggestion. They believed that syphilis originated in Germany because of an apparent outbreak there. For this reason, the Spanish called syphilis the "German Disease." Syphilis took on many other names as it spread throughout the world. The Dutch also called it "Spanish Disease" while the Russians attributed the disease to the Polish. Its spread by British sailors to the Pacific islands gave it the name "British Disease" among the residents of Tahiti. Disputes between Christians and Turkish Muslims gave syphilis the name "Christian Disease" among the Turks. The idea of naming syphilis after an enemy was due to the perception that syphilis was caused by immoral acts, such as prostitution and indecent acts with animals.

German author and revolutionary Ulrich von Hutten (1488–1523) admitted to having syphilis in his writings. Few would publicly acknowledge having the disease in that era. Von Hutten explained how the disease affected his body and described his encounters with the different types of treatments. His accounts were more accurate and detailed than the medical writings of the time. Descriptions of painful boils and dark green pus from ulcerated skin horrified the afflicted and unafflicted alike.

Syphilis spread rapidly throughout Europe despite its name and uncertain origins. Many Europeans blamed the

Figure 2.2 Christopher Columbus and Native Americans in the New World. Syphilis was seen as a curse on the explorers for their maltreatment of the Native Americans. Accounts of sexual encounters between the crew and the native people are well documented. (Library of Congress)

unrestrained spread of syphilis on the Gauls, who are now known as the French. It was believed that the troops of King Charles VIII of France introduced syphilis everywhere else in

Europe. King Charles used paid soldiers from various regions of Europe. It was alleged that the soldiers brought syphilis back to their homelands after serving in Charles's army. Syphilis then took on the title of "French Disease," or *morbus gallicus*, adding to its repertoire of names.

The modern term *syphilis* as we know it came about in 1530, upon the publication of a poem called *Syphilis save morgues Gallicus* by Italian physician Girolamo Fracastoro. His fictional character Syphilis, a romantic shepherd in the mythical story, was claimed to have originated the scourge. Syphilis's sinister deeds, and not his sexual activity, brought about the disease as punishment. Thus, the shepherd Syphilis's name became slang for the disease.

By 1600 most of the parts of the world that had been visited by conquerors, traders, and travelers suffered from syphilis. Its swift spread, spanning mountains and oceans, bewildered the clergy and medical community alike. European clergy at the time attributed the disease to God's fury against sinners. Prophets and priests in other regions blamed astronomical phenomena and a host of other causes. The explanations given by physicians were no more accurate than those of the clergy. Even more misleading was the fact that many medical practitioners called the new disease the "new plague" or "pox." These erroneous appellations caused people to confuse the malady with black plague and smallpox. In spite of disagreements about its origin and cause, almost all agreed that the disease was associated with an illicit activity, usually sex. Prostitution was recognized as means of spreading the disease, which resulted in restrictions on the practice. In some countries, prostitutes were often required to identify themselves with some unique type of clothing or accessory.

The fact that syphilis was confused with many other diseases led nineteenth-century physician Sir William Osler to call syphilis the "Great Imposter" or the "Great Masquerader."

American physicians encountering what they thought was syphilis during that period simply called it "bad blood." The terms "bad blood" or "plague" were commonly used to describe deadly diseases of unknown origins. Unfortunately, physicians of the time had few ways to distinguish between the different diseases. Confusion and disagreement among physicians and scientists were common.

Syphilis's dishonorable history has fueled many debates, from its first discovery up until today. Scholars of the initial period of syphilis outbreaks, such as English novelist Gideon Harvey, had heated arguments about the arrival of syphilis in Europe. No one wanted the disease attributed to his or her national origin or culture. What started out as rational explanations for its origination turned into finger pointing based on political viewpoints. For example, Harvey attributed the French's "slovenly sexual attitudes" to the origin of syphilis. William Shakespeare even took part in the syphilis debate, calling it the "French Disease" in many of his works. Literary scholars believed he did this to poke fun at the French during the Anglo-French Wars.

There are passages in early Greek and Roman literature indicating that syphilis may have been in Europe long before Columbus returned from the New World. In addition, treatments for a disease known as "venereal leprosy" were reported in twelfth-century medical documents. The medication only worked for venereal leprosy, meaning that the disease was not being confused with true leprosy. Archeologists studying these accounts believe that venereal leprosy was confused with **yaws**, a condition related to syphilis. Yaws may have been brought back from Greek and Roman settlements in North Africa and the Middle East. Others believe that ancient Hebrew circumcision practices were linked to lower rates of **sexually transmitted diseases** such as syphilis. This was based on observations that Jewish populations had fewer cases of syphilis than Christians. In 1983 a Canadian medical report provided evidence to the beliefs of some historians that the ancient Hebrew circumcision practices were linked to lower rates of sexually transmitted diseases such as syphilis.[1]

THE TABOO OF SYPHILIS

Unlike other disease outbreaks occurring between 1500 and 1600, syphilis spread subtly and showed up in a variety of ways. Many people had mild symptoms and spread the disease, not knowing they were infected. Others quickly succumbed to syphilis, developing severe ailments that sometimes resulted in death. Most people who showed even the earliest signs of syphilis were shunned. Physicians were even repulsed by syphilis patients and many avoided touching them. Hospitals throughout Europe refused to admit syphilis patients, fearing proliferation of the disease throughout the facility and community.

The meager hospital care that was available to syphilis patients was pathetic and despicable even by early European standards. Nearly all patients ended up in crowded wards and got little care or treatment. The wards were merely a space to live out the course of the disease until death. Luckier patients were assigned to leprosy clinics and mental health institutions where they at least received some comfort. Treatment of syphilis varied, much of it associated with atonement for sin. Syphilis was not the only disease attributed to sinfulness. Other common diseases of that period were said to be caused by evil thoughts, inappropriate touching, foul moods, laziness, and dirty and unkempt living conditions.

Reports of the disease were tainted by the disdain for it. Physicians generally included statements such as "revolting sores" and "foul pus" in their descriptions. Patients were often described as "loathsome" or declared to be involved in "acts of debauchery." Descriptions of the disease overlapped

SYPHILIS AND CREATIVITY

Many people suffered from syphilis throughout history. Few were bold enough to admit having the disease. The stigma of syphilis took a brief hiatus from the mid 1800s through the early 1900s. Those individuals whose condition was public were noted for being some of the most creative, and in many cases eccentric, people in society. A cadre of famous French artists and writers used syphilis as a badge of their passion for life. Included were the illustrious artists Edgar Degas, Paul Gauguin, Édouard Manet, Henri de Toulouse-Lautrec, and Vincent van Gogh. However, few knew that nineteenth-century Irish writer Oscar Wilde lamented of syphilis, believing he had captured this disease from romance and free spirit. Apparently, he believed that his escapades warranted having the disease.

Wilde, like many of the creative afflicted, even partook of absinthe, a strong alcoholic beverage, commonly thought to be a cure for syphilis. However, friends and physicians quickly recognized that Wilde was suffering from other ailments probably related to absinthe poisoning. The fact that he never showed sores and had chronically itchy skin revealed the condition as not being syphilis.

A comtemporary of Wilde, American chess genius Harry Pillsbury, endured syphilis. Pillsbury was the most articulate chess and checkers player, renowned for playing 20 competitors at one time and beating all the top masters of the era. Like the other artists, his troubled creativity was linked to syphilis, which killed him at the age of 34. Billionaire Howard Hughes also suffered from syphilis. It is believed that the disease contributed to his mental decline, leaving him with eccentricities that included a fear of germs, the need to be an extreme recluse, and an obsession with saving his urine.

those of other conditions beleaguering Europe. This made accurate **diagnosis** and **therapy** difficult. It was not until the 1800s that physicians starting making sense of syphilis.

Three hundred years of ignorance about syphilis were stripped away when scientists identified **microorganisms** as the cause of **infectious** disease. Unlike many other diseases, syphilis still retained an ignoble role in history because of its sexual transmission.

Syphilis remained a mysterious malady even up to the nineteenth century in England and the United States. In the late 1800s, death and **morbidity** from syphilis were still escalating. The philosophy of Victorian England produced a belief that syphilis was spread only among "lower-class" people, including prostitutes. For a brief period, prostitution in Europe was strictly regulated to prevent lower-class people from infecting the aristocrats. After all, the nobility believed that dignified people could acquire syphilis but not pass it along. Prostitutes with syphilis were jailed while noblemen with the disease were spared incarceration. Other European countries followed this bias by mandating the registration and inspection of prostitutes in an attempt to reduce syphilis.

Not all people shunned syphilis. For some men, syphilis became a label of amorous conquests. It meant that the person had been successful at securing many sexual partners. Rebellious people who opposed the contemporary morality also considered syphilis an emblem of protest. Famous people who were noted for numerous affairs were usually labeled syphilitic whether or not they had the disease.

VAMPIRISM AND SYPHILIS

Vampires are part of a fanciful ancient myth that is still pervasive in modern movies and television shows. The contemporary view of vampires comes from Bram Stoker's famous novel *Dracula*. However, the idea of vampires, humans, or other creatures that subsist on blood predates the Old Testament.

One might wonder why vampires are being included in a discussion of the history of syphilis. Much like syphilis, vampirism was used as a symbol of social deviance, especially for out-of-the-ordinary behaviors related to sexuality. Many literary scholars believe that vampirism was used by Victorian-era writers to represent the grip of syphilis on society. Vampires and syphilis were both perceived as ruinous to society. Both seemed to defy Christian morality. In addition, many stories portray vampirism as **contagious**. It spread from the vampire to an unfortunate victim, usually through an unnatural act such as puncturing the victim's body with teeth. Vampirism passed from one person to another in much the same way that syphilis was alleged to spread through aberrant behavior.

Public panic over syphilis and other diseases led to the widespread murder of people accused of vampirism. Unfortunate people with a variety of debilitating diseases, including advanced syphilis, were labeled as vampires and killed to prevent further spread of the disease. A variety of methods were developed to kill vampires. Each method was created from a combination of local and borrowed folklore about the elimination of ungodly creatures. Dead people accused of vampirism had to be exhumed and disposed of according to the traditions of killing vampires. Today, certain vampirism groups drink the blood of animals and humans as a religious practice. Whether these practices spread disease is not well documented.

FAMOUS PEOPLE AND SYPHILIS

Dishonorable nicknames and titles given to famous people go far back in human history. This, and the assigning of certain diseases to these people, was an effective way of discrediting foes, scoundrels, and incompetent leaders. However, few diseases gained the high stature of syphilis in being associated with noteworthy people.

Christopher Columbus was the first famous European accused of having syphilis. His detractors blamed him for seeking sexual favors with the American Indians. He was

Figure 2.3 King Henry VIII of England may have suffered from syphilis; historians have theorized that this disease might explain the degree of trouble Henry VIII and his wives had producing children. (© Réunion des Musées Nationaux/Art Resource, NY)

thereby blamed for introducing syphilis to Europe. However, there is no evidence in Columbus's highly chronicled life that he suffered from syphilis. Most historians believe he was a scapegoat. His crew, however, most likely carried syphilis back to Europe. Accounts of sexual encounters between the crew and the native people are well documented. Syphilis was

Figure 2.4 Anne Boleyn, second wife of Henry VIII, was accused of adultery and having passed syphilis on to her husband. These accusations were leveled against her because she had produced no male heir and Henry wanted a quick divorce. However, the accusation of adultery led to Anne's beheading in 1536. (© Réunion des Musées Nationaux/Art Resource, NY)

considered a curse on the crew because of their cruel treatment of the Indians.

The most esteemed person said to have succumbed to the effects of syphilis was sixteenth century English King Henry VIII.

Henry VIII had difficulties producing children with all of his six wives. Many of his wives' pregnancies ended in miscarriages or stillbirths, and several of his children died very young; these are all things that can happen when women with untreated syphilis become pregnant. Although infant mortality was high in the sixteenth century, historians have theorized that a disease like syphilis might help explain the degree of trouble Henry VIII and his wives had producing children. Claims of Henry VIII's syphilitic condition were also attributable in part to his insanity. Many historians speculate that he died with his brain destroyed by syphilis.

Syphilis was said to have molded the life and art of nineteenth-century Dutch artist Vincent van Gogh. Combined

Figure 2.5 Al Capone died of complications of syphilis in 1947. (© AP Images)

with his apparent depression, the disease was claimed to be responsible for Van Gogh's despair and eccentricity. Much of his art reflected both conditions. According to many artists, Van Gogh's works took on the progressive hopelessness of his life as the disease advanced and worsened his health. Van Gogh committed suicide before any of his medical conditions could be confirmed.

Chicago gangster Al Capone (1899–1947) was one of the most notorious syphilitics. He is one of the few mentioned here whose case was confirmed by medical examination. Capone began showing symptoms of the disease while serving a jail sentence for tax evasion.

Henri de Toulouse-Lautrec, the nineteenth-century French artist, was known for the birth defects leading to his dwarfism and twisted body stature. Others claimed that he was sickly and weak because of family inbreeding. His parents were first cousins. Toulouse-Lautrec's fondness for brothels resulted in his contracting the syphilis that apparently shortened his life.

Other famous people who supposedly had syphilis were French emperor Napoleon Bonaparte (1769–1821), French painter and revolutionary Édouard Manet (1832–1883), French painter Paul Gauguin (1848–1903), French poet Arthur Rimbaud (1855–1891), Austrian composer Hugo Wolf (1860–1903), German philosopher Friedrich Wilhelm Nietzsche (1844–1900), Austrian composer Franz Schubert (1797–1828), and American billionaire Howard Hughes (1905–1976). Many of these cases cannot be confirmed because of the lack of medical evidence.

3

Syphilis: From Plague to STD

Co-morbidity, or illness due to simultaneous infections with two or more diseases, is turning out to be very common with syphilis. An initial study of sexually transmitted disease (STD) co-infections was carried out between 1999 and 2001 in California. The study was prompted by an abundance of coinfection reports while investigating patients initially diagnosed with one type of STD. Out of 1,039 syphilis cases, researchers found that 77 percent of people diagnosed with syphilis were discovered to have AIDS. The comorbidity rate of STDs steadily increased from 1999 to 2001. Current disease reports from around the world indicate that co-morbidity with syphilis is still very common. It has become a standard practice to look for other infections when investigating any diagnosed STDs.[1]

Syphilis was not always recognized as a sexually transmitted disease (STD). Cultural taboos, misconceptions, and myths hid the facts of how the disease was really transmitted. Finally, scrutiny and consistent observations of the disease by early physicians confirmed that it was spread primarily through sexual contact. It was not until later in history that the scientific community recognized it as a disease caused by a microorganism invading the body.

It was the initial use of the microscope in 1665 by English scientist Robert Hooke that led scientists to the road of discovering the organic basis of disease. Around the same time in Holland, Dutch amateur scientist Anton van Leeuwenhoek became the first person to see microorganisms, which he labeled animacules. However, scientists and society did

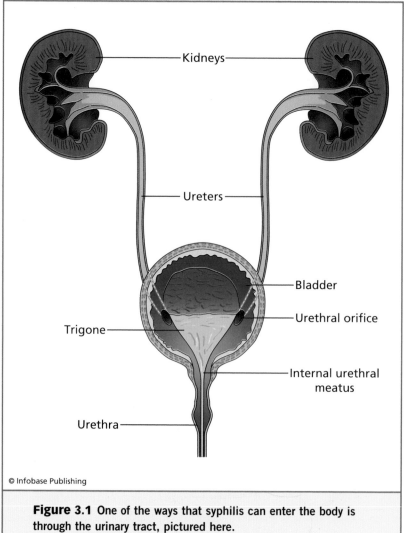

© Infobase Publishing

Figure 3.1 One of the ways that syphilis can enter the body is through the urinary tract, pictured here.

not accept the fact that organisms could cause disease until the meticulous research of Italian physician Francesco Redi and French chemist Louis Pasteur in the mid-1800s demonstrated this fact.

WHAT IS AN STD?

Physicians and scientists characterize STDs as one category of **genitourinary**, or **urogenital** infections. This includes microorganisms that enter the body through the urinary tract and reproductive system. Urinary tract infections are usually local-

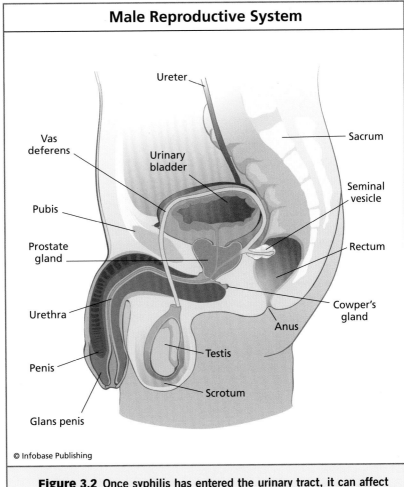

Male Reproductive System

© Infobase Publishing

Figure 3.2 Once syphilis has entered the urinary tract, it can affect all parts of the urinary and reproductive systems. This is the male reproductive system.

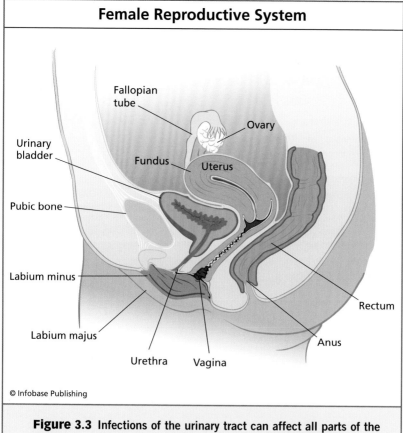

Female Reproductive System

Fallopian tube

Ovary

Urinary bladder

Fundus

Uterus

Pubic bone

Labium minus

Rectum

Labium majus

Anus

Urethra

Vagina

© Infobase Publishing

Figure 3.3 Infections of the urinary tract can affect all parts of the urinary and reproductive systems. This is the female reproductive system.

ized to the urethra, urinary bladder, ureters, and kidneys (Figure 3.1). Genital tract infections can attack the urinary tract but affect the reproductive system as well. In males, this may include the penis, vas deferens, and testicles. Infections in females can cause problems to the vagina, cervix, uterus, fallopian tubes, and ovaries.

Today it is commonly accepted that microscopic creatures called microorganisms cause genitourinary infections. The types of **microorganisms** that cause genitourinary infections are bacteria, **fungi**, **protozoa**, and viruses. Bacteria are primitive, minuscule single-celled organisms that generally feed by breaking down decaying and living material. They are found almost everywhere on Earth, even in our own bodies and in the bodies of other creatures. Most bacteria cause no harm. However, there are many pathogenic bacteria that cause disease in animals, plants, and people. The microorganism causing syphilis belongs to this category of living things.

For many people the term fungus evokes a variety of images, ranging from mushrooms that cause allergies to the colorful growth found on foods left too long in the refrigerator. Fungi are comprised of an assorted group of organisms that generally grow as strands of cells called a mycelium. They feed by breaking down

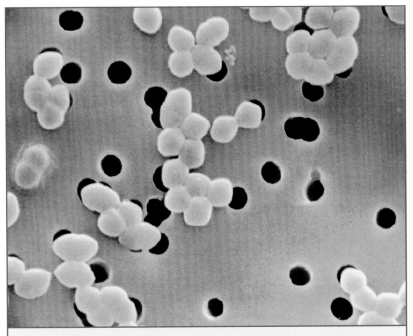

Figure 3.4 Bacteria are tiny, single-celled organisms, similar to those pictured here. Some bacteria are harmful, but most are harmless or even helpful to the body. (Centers for Disease Control and Prevention/ Janice Carr)

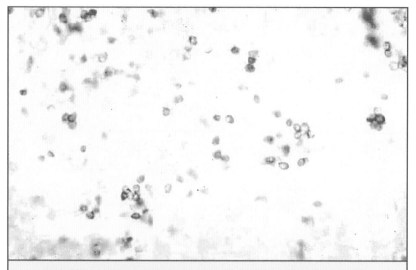

Figure 3.5 Fungi take many shapes, such as mushrooms, mold, and yeast. Here, yeast grows in culture on a Petri dish. (Centers for Disease Control and Prevention)

decaying complex matter. Like bacteria, some are pathogens and cause disease as they invade the bodies of living organisms.

Protozoa are complex, single-celled organisms that live like animals or plants. They are identified by the way they move around. Some crawl, using structures called pseudopods, while others swim, propelled by whip-like parts called cilia and flagella. Most protozoa cause few disease problems for people. Nevertheless, there are pathogenic ones that cause devastating diseases in animals and people. Malaria and sleeping sickness are two protozoan diseases that are responsible for numerous deaths in Africa, Asia, Southern Europe, and South America. A protozoan called *Trypanosoma* causes African sleeping sickness.

Viruses are the ultimate disease-causing organism. There are no known viruses that do not cause some type of disease. Almost any living organism is susceptible to viral diseases. Viruses attack bacteria, fungi, protozoa, plants, and animals. Some even tag along as uninvited guests of other viruses, living off the host virus's activity. Scientists disagree as to whether viruses are living organisms. They lack all the structures found in other creatures and can only survive on the metabolism of their host. Therefore, they can only live within the cells of a host organism. Their makeup is no more complex than a small piece of genetic material covered by a protein capsule.

As a rule, harmless microorganisms inhabit specific parts of the urinary tract and reproductive system of humans. For example, the vagina normally has beneficial lactobacilli bacteria that reduce the chances of assault by pathogenic microorganisms. Fungi called vaginal yeast also reside in the vagina. Males are usually free of genitourinary microorganisms except for at the extreme end of the urethra, where typically harmless bacteria such as *Corynebacterium, Haemophilus, Lactobacillis, Staphylococcus,* and *Streptococcus* are found. Much of the urinary tract and reproductive system is kept free of invasion

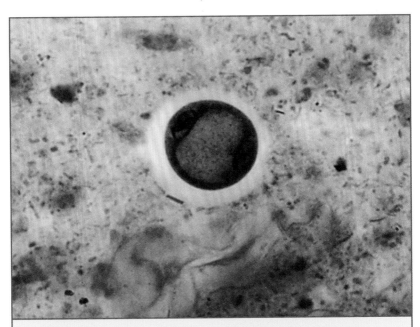

Figure 3.6 Protozoa, like bacteria, are single-celled organisms. Protozoa are much more complex than bacterial cells and are defined by the way they move in their environment. (Centers for Disease Control and Prevention)

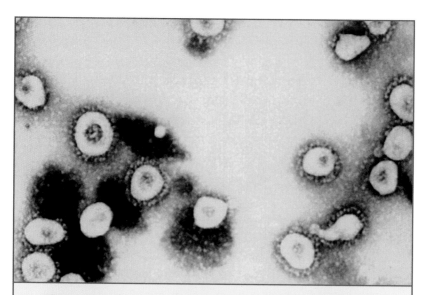

Figure 3.7 Viruses are unlike any other pathogen. They lack all structures found in other organisms and cannot live without feeding off their host. They are much smaller than bacteria and composed only of genetic material in a protein capsule. (Centers for Disease Control and Prevention)

from pathogenic microorganisms by a variety of effective body defenses.

An STD occurs when microorganisms in the genitourinary system produce illness by breaching the body's defense mechanisms. **Opportunistic** STDs occur when the normal genitourinary inhabitants get out of control, producing illness. This can happen when they accidentally enter other parts of the urinary tract and reproductive system. Disease can also occur if the person's **immune system** is weakened. The immune system then cannot prevent these microorganisms from overpopulating and subsequently causing discomfort and ailments. Even when the immune system is functioning, sometimes simple conditions such as a lack of urine flow can allow genitourinary microorganisms to cause disease.

STDs commonly result when **pathogens,** or microorganisms, enter the urinary tract and reproductive system. This usually occurs during sexual activity. Syphilis is one of many microorganisms causing this kind of STD.

TYPES OF STDs

Urinary tract infections caused by intestinal bacteria are probably the most common although least diagnosed type of STD. *Escherichia coli*, an ordinary denizen of the large intestine, regularly makes its way to the penis and vagina through sexual contact. It accounts for approximately 60 percent of the diagnosed urinary tract infections. The percentage of *Escherichia coli* infections caused by sexual contact is unknown. Other intestinal bacteria that commonly cause urinary tract infections include *Enterobacter aeroginosa, Pseudomonas aeruginosa*, and various species of *Proteus*. Luckily, these infections are usually short lived and easy to treat with conventional medications.

Gonorrhea is an STD caused by a pathogenic bacterium called *Neisseria gonorrhoeae*. It is from a family of bacteria that can cause ear infections, sore throats, and even meningitis in children and young adults. Gonorrhea ranks with syphilis as one of the most common STDs. Military physicians in the United States and Europe noted outbreaks of gonorrhea during World War I. The disease was difficult to diagnosis earlier in history because it was overshadowed by syphilis infections. Gonorrhea is usually more evident in males because it causes painful urination as the organism inflames the urethra and vas deferens. The disease is not always as noticeable and symptomatic in females. Many women do not feel any pain or discomfort while the bacteria travel from the vagina up to the fallopian tubes. This asymptomatic spread of the disease creates a dangerous situation because the disease can go untreated, resulting in **pelvic inflammatory disease (PID)**, which can cause **infertility** or death.

Commonly confused with gonorrhea, the STD known as **chlamydia** surprised the medical community with its high rate of prevalence (the number of cases of a disease that are present in a population at a specified time). The disease is caused by an unusual parasitic bacterium called *Chlamydia trachomatis*. Symptoms in males and females are very similar to those of gonorrhea and often are misdiagnosed in males and undetected in females. Studies done on sexually active college students in the 1990s showed that an alarming number of students were carrying and spreading the microorganism. The disease can spread to children during vaginal childbirth, causing eye and respiratory infections. Unchecked chlamydial infections produce the same end results as untreated gonorrhea. Unfortunately, many college-age students can become infertile if they do not take measures to prevent getting STDs or do not seek STD testing.

Chancroid is a little known STD caused by the pathogenic bacterium *Haemophilus ducreyi*. Related bacteria cause eye infections and respiratory disease in animals and people. Many *Haemophilus* diseases, including chancroid, were derived from domesticated animals. It is unusual for diseases of animals to spread to humans as a new type of disease. The disease is prevalent in developing nations, particularly in tropical regions where it can infect whole communities. Prostitutes in major urban areas spread most cases of chancroid in the United States and Europe. It produces sores similar to those produced by syphilis and was probably mistaken for syphilis before it was positively identified. However, unlike the sores of syphilis, chancroid sores are painful. Chancroid is on the rise and currently can be treated with **antibiotics**.

Bacterial **vaginosis**, or irritation of the vaginal tract, is a mysterious STD. Considering the amount of technology available for studying disease, little is known about the cause of bacterial vaginosis. Cases of the disease show a host of pathogens and naturally occurring bacteria. The disease is usually found in sexually active women, meaning that most likely it is an STD. Common antibiotics are used to treat the condition, which is often diagnosed along with syphilis.

A normally benign fungus that inhabits the intestines and vagina causes an infection almost exclusive to females. *Candida albicans*, a single-celled fungus called a yeast, produces a disease called candidiasis. **Candidiasis** can cause disease in the mouth, skin, and nails; however, it is most noted for creating problems in the female reproductive system. Candidiasis can produce a variety of problems ranging from vaginal itching to irritating vaginal discharges. Most cases are not severe and can be cured with antifungal drugs. Antibiotic treatment will aggravate the disease by killing off the normal bacteria in the GI tract, allowing overgrowth of the yeast. Candidiasis in males is rare and is usually limited to the surface of the penis. It is easily treated with prescription antifungal creams.

Trichomoniasis, caused by *Trichomonas vaginalis,* is probably the least known STD to most people. Yet, it is one of the most common causes of vaginal discomfort resulting from sexual contact. A pathogenic protozoan found throughout the world causes the disease. It is related to the organisms causing sleeping sickness and conditions leading to the decay of bone, cartilage, and skin. As with candidiasis and vaginitis, trichomoniasis is mostly found in females. The disease causes severe vaginal itching and extremely painful urination. It is usually apparent because the vagina produces a foamy yellow-green discharge. Infections in males can go undetected. This is just the opposite of gonorrhea, which is most evident in males. However, some males may feel discomfort and suffer pain in the testicles. The condition can be treated with medication. Trichomoniasis is common alone, but can be found with other common STDs such as syphilis and gonorrhea.

Viruses also plague the urinary tract and reproductive system. The most common of the viral STDs is **genital herpes**. People who have the disease know it when small painful blisters appear around the vagina or penis. These blisters are very similar to those found with cold sores and chicken pox. That is because related viruses cause these three diseases. Genital **herpes** starts out with severe symptoms, leaving the person with ulcers created by the virus as it reproduces in the skin and urinary tract lining. The blisters then become infrequent and less severe as the disease progresses. It is a lifelong disease that often accompanies other STDs. Prevention is the best precaution. Antiviral treatments

SYPHILIS AND FOOD— AN UNUSUAL ASSOCIATION

Today it is commonly accepted that syphilis is generally spread by sexual contact. However, this was not true before the discovery of its bacterial origins. Initially, most people supposed syphilis was caused by sinful behavior or thoughts. This was consistent with the overall belief model of human disease.

However, few diseases got the reputation of being caused by eating a particular food. Many people in seventeenth-century Europe attributed syphilis, as well as other diseases such as leprosy, to the then lowly potato. Europeans first encountered potatoes during the Spanish explorations of Peru in the 1500s. Pedro Cieza de Leon noticed the natives dining on a variety of potatoes and used them to feed his conquistadors. The connection of potatoes to syphilis helped explain the introduction of the disease into Europe. Archeological records show that Aymara Indians cultivated potatoes before A.D. 400. The Central and South American Indians regularly traded potatoes. To many of the Indians, the potato was a symbol of surplus and was incorporated into art and pottery. However, to many fifteenth-century Europeans, the potato was viewed as repulsive and dangerous. After all, it was botanically related to a poisonous plant called the deadly nightshade.

For the same reason, tomatoes were also considered deadly during that period. Potatoes were eventually freed from the stigma of syphilis as it became cultivated throughout Europe in the 1600s and 1700s.

such as acyclovir do not remove the virus from the body. Rather, they reduce the incidence of blister flare-ups. People with the disease can spread it the rest of their lives. It is possible to spread the disease even if the person has no current signs or symptoms.

The STD called **genital warts** is caused by the human papillomavirus. It is related to the viruses causing warts commonly found on the hands and feet. Genital warts are exclusively spread by sexual contact. In males, the disease appears as lumpy growths, usually located near the tip of the penis. The warts are usually painless and must be removed by surgery. There is no cure for this disease. Removing the warts surgically does not rid the body of the virus and does not reduce its frequency. Females also develop warts on the **genitals**. In addition to the warts, viruses located on the cervix can lead to a fatal disease called cervical cancer. Surgery and chemotherapy treatments are available for the cervical cancer stage. As with many of the other STDs mentioned, genital warts are frequently found with other STDs. A human papillomavirus (HPV) vaccine is now available to protect against genital warts. It can reduce the incidence of genital warts by 90 percent and cervical cancer by 70 percent. It has been proposed that all young women be vaccinated before their first sexual activity to reduce the chance of cervical cancer. A similar vaccine is being developed to protect against herpes viruses.

The most famous, or rather infamous, viral STD is acquired immunodeficiency syndrome (**AIDS)**. Caused by the **human immunodeficiency virus**, (HIV), AIDS is the most ruthless and fatal STD. The virus primarily gains access to the body through sexual contact. It then travels to the bloodstream and lymph nodes, where it degrades the immune system. People do not directly die from the virus. Their weakened immune system makes them susceptible to other infections, some of which can lead to cancer. Current AIDS treatments do not cure the disease. Rather, they slow down its progress, prolonging the victim's life. AIDS is commonly found with bacterial STDs such as chlamydial infection, gonorrhea, and syphilis.

HOW DO THEY SPREAD?

Circumstances ranging from inappropriate touching of the genitals, toilet seats, and bathing in a dirty bathtub have been implicated in the spread of STDs. However, most of the microorganisms causing STDs do not survive well out of the host's body. Therefore, it is unlikely that objects or water can spread them. *Trichomonas* is probably the most likely candidate for being spread by objects. There is some evidence that the organism can survive for a short period on moist towels, undergarments, and feminine hygiene napkins. Unclean instruments used for gynecologic and rectal examinations may also pose a risk of STD spread. Most STD microorganisms are killed by exposure to air and light. The air in many buildings and houses is kept dry by air conditioning or heating. This dehydrates the microorganisms, rendering them incapable of surviving for long. Sunlight and bright indoor lights may destroy the microorganisms' genetic material, thereby reducing their chance of reproducing. These are not very likely models of transmission.

Most STDs are spread just as their name suggests, through sexual contact, specifically genital contact. Avoiding sexual activity, and using condoms during sexual contact, are the best ways to prevent acquiring one of these infections. Note that most STDs are found in conjunction with another STD. Scientists believe that having one STD predisposes the body to others. A weakening of the body's antimicrobial defense mechanisms is the most probable explanation for this observation. Casual touching and kissing are unlikely methods of spreading most STDs. The microorganisms usually enter the body through the urinary tract and reproductive system during sexual intercourse. This makes females more vulnerable to getting STDs. The anatomy of the female reproductive system reduces the chance that the microorganisms will be flushed out by urination after sexual contact. Some physicians believe that uncircumcised males have an increased chance of acquiring STDs. It is thought that the microorganisms can be hidden and protected under the folds of the foreskin. STDs are equally likely to enter the body through the mouth and rectum through oral or anal sexual contact. Many cases of AIDS and syphilis were most likely acquired this way. STDs that invade the blood, such as AIDS and syphilis, are readily transmitted through fresh blood contact. This may occur through needle sharing, transfusion with contaminated blood, and careless handling of blood from infected people.

4

Treponema Pallidum: The Syphilis Organism

Dr. Mary Francis got the blood tests back for a 25-year-old male patient she referred to as Oscar. Oscar was officially diagnosed with syphilis and may have picked it up during an extended stay in Thailand. He admitted that he had probably contracted syphilis from prostitutes in the city of Patong. Oscar is lucky that he was diagnosed early and will be treated before the disease becomes fatal. Throughout the world many people are dying from the complications of syphilis. A 2004 World Health Organization report about syphilis death rates showed that 43,000 people died from syphilis in Southeast Asia, compared to Africa with 89,000 deaths and the United States with 1,000 deaths.[1]

The microorganism causing syphilis is a bacterium called *Treponema pallidum*, which belongs to a group of bacteria called **spirochetes**. Their name comes from their spiral shape. These usually large and elaborately shaped bacteria are able to wiggle themselves in a rigid, wormlike manner using structures not found in other bacteria. Spirochetes caught the eye of Anton van Leeuwenhoek in 1683. He was the first person to view them during the microscopic examination of saliva samples. They comprise a widespread group of organisms found in water, soil, and the bodies of other creatures. However, most spirochetes have exacting environmental requirements, making them difficult to grow in the laboratory. Therefore many have to be studied in their natural environments. Not every spiral-shaped bacterium is a spirochete. A helical bacterium called *Spirilla volutans* resembles spirochetes but is unrelated. This interesting bacterium is

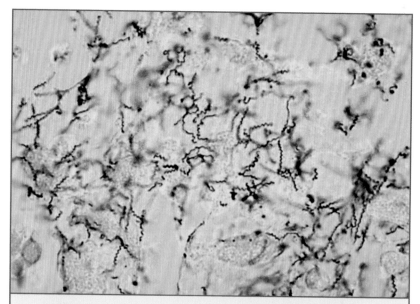

Figure 4.1 *Treponema pallidum* is the bacterium that causes syphilis. It has a spiral shape as can be seen in this picture, and is thus classified as a spirochete bacterium. (Centers for Disease Control and Prevention/Dr. Edwin P. Ewing, Jr.)

harvested from fresh water as a food for animals and humans. Many health food and vegetarian stores sell spirullum food products.

Treponema is named for its shape, which looks like a twisting, pulsating thread. They were named by Fritz Schaudinn, who discovered and researched several mysterious deadly infectious diseases that plagued people in the 1880s. *Treponema* belongs to a collection of spirochetes noted for causing diseases in plants, animals, and humans. *Borrelia burgdorferi* is a spirochete found in several types of blood-sucking relatives of spiders called ticks. Relatives of this bacterium infect a large variety of insects and other arthropods that suck sap or feed on blood. Over the past 20 years, *Borrelia burgdorferi* has come under the scrutiny of scientists and public health officials. The organism causes a condition called Lyme disease when it enters humans. *Borrelia burgdorferi* enters the body through the bite of an infected deer tick. It proceeds throughout the body causing **fever**, joint pain, and even paralysis. Deer are known to carry *Borrelia burgdorferi* without showing any significant signs of disease. Another dangerous spirochete is *Leptospira interrogans.* It is noted for a type of food poisoning called leptospirosis. It is regularly found in the kidneys of domesticated animals. The organism exits the animal through the urine, making it possible to be spread through contaminated soil and water. *Serpula* and *Serpulina*, which are often misclassified as *Treponema*, are intestinal spirochetes of many mammals. They are confirmed to cause diarrheal diseases in pigs. Little else is known about these organisms.

BIOLOGY AND NATURAL HISTORY OF TREPONEMA

All *Treponema* organisms cause some type of mild to severe disease in humans. Even though different species of *Treponema* cause distinctly dissimilar diseases, they all share a common signature of bone scarring after the long-term infection has ravaged the body. This bone scarring was noted in early examinations of syphilitic **cadavers**. Bone abnormalities are now routinely studied by archeologists to assess diseases in ancient humans. Similar studies are done on animals to see if their diseases could have spread to humans. Unfortunately, the bone scarring does not allow the archeologists to distinguish between the different types of *Treponema*. In addition, the scarring must be found on a number of bones to avoid confusion with other conditions that could scar individual bones. Some distinction between the different *Treponema* species is possible because syphilis alone produces scars on the skull bones. It makes the skull appear to have been chewed on by worms. This scarring pattern is called *caries sicca.*

The classification of bacteria is an ongoing and ever-changing process. Microbiologists generally agree that human *Treponema* organisms can be categorized in at least seven distinct

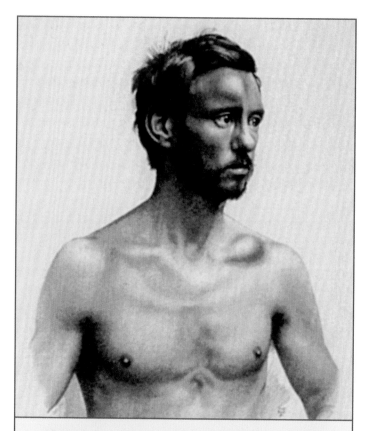

Figure 4.2 *Treponema* organisms can cause many diseases, and not all of the diseases have visible symptoms at all stages. This becomes evident in the picture of the man, above, who has tertiary syphilis but does not show any physical signs or symptoms. However, *Treponema* can cause internal problems such as gummas and bone scarring. (National Library of Medicine)

species: *T. amylovorum, T. carateum, T. denticola, T. lecithino-lyticum, T. maltophilum, T. pallidum,* and *T. socranskii.* Syphilis is associated with *T. pallidum. T. pallidum* is further divided into specific categories called serotypes, strains, or subspecies. These subcategories are determined by studying the chemistry of the organism's cell and by analyzing the genetic material.

Different types of *T. pallidum* affect the body in distinctive ways. Many microbiologists classify *T. pallidum* into three traditional subcategories: *T. pallidum endemicum, T. pallidum pallidum,* and *T. pallidum pertenue*. It is believed that *T. pallidum pertenue* is actually a separate organism that should be categorized as *T. pertenue.*

Genetic studies are continually being performed on *Treponema* bacteria as a means of better treating syphilis treatments. New research indicates that the *Treponema* that caused syphilis in 1500s Europe was not the same strain commonly found to cause syphilis today. In addition, the strains of *Treponema* causing syphilis are likely dissimilar in different parts of world.

For years dentists have had evidence the *Treponema* bacteria were regular inhabitants of the human mouth. They usually reside on the gums and are considered harmless. In 1997, *T. amylovorum* was discovered to damage the gums, causing a condition called **periodontal** disease. This particular *Treponema* species feeds on sugars that accumulate in the mouth after eating. It is primarily seen in people with poor dental hygiene practices. Further research in the later 1990s and early 2000s shows the presence of other oral *Treponema* associated with various gum and tooth diseases. These different types of *Treponema* do not compete with *T. amylovorum* because they eat other components of food that remains in the mouth after a meal. However, most of them thrive on diets high in **carbohydrates**. The new ones include *T. denticola, T. lecithinolyticum, T. matlophilum, T. parvum, T. pectinovorum,* and *T. socranskii.* A very severe form of gum disease is caused by *T. putidum.* It causes the gums to rot away, exposing the jawbones to damage.

T. carateum causes a little-known disease called **pinta**. The organism is very difficult to distinguish from any of the *T. pallidum* strains. Pinta is found only in isolated parts of Central America, Colombia, and the southernmost tip of Mexico. The disease is limited to rural areas. Often called a nonvenereal treponematosis, pinta is recognized by the large patches of flat, red skin lesions that form within months after infection. The lesions are most likely to appear on the scalp, feet, and hands. Pinta is usually contracted during childhood and remains for the life of the person. It is spread by direct contact. People with the pinta skin lesions can pass the disease to unaffected people by casual touch. One contact is probably not enough to spread the disease. Most likely it is spread by continuous contact between family members. Bones are rarely scarred by pinta because *T. carateum* confines its attack to the skin.

Bejel, or endemic syphilis, is a condition similar to pinta in many ways but is caused by *T. pallidum endemicum*. This disease is also found among isolated populations of people living in warm regions. However, bejel is primarily confined to the Middle East. Bejel, like pinta, starts during youth by continuous contact with infected family members and friends. It first appears as a small red lesion at the point where it has entered the body. Unlike pinta, bejel typically infects the skin of the mouth and may progress to the nose and throat lining. Therefore, it is spread by contact with shared drinking and eating utensils as well as direct contact with lesions. This disease can spread beyond the skin to the heart and nervous system, causing premature death. It also can spread to infants during childbirth as a condition called **congenital** endemic syphilis. Bone scarring does occur with this disease, especially later in life.

Yaws, also caused by a nonvenereal *Treponema*, is believed to be the closest relative to syphilis. It is found worldwide, predominantly in rural areas of tropical regions. It is caused by *T. pallidum pertenue*. The bacterium starts out by causing a large, red, painless lesion called the mother yaw. It appears approximately one month after infection. This initial condition is similar to bejel. The mother yaw lesion ulcerates and later heals, making it seem that the disease has left the body. Usually, a large reddened patch of skin persists around the mother yaw lesion. Other lesions then start to appear all over the body within months or years after the initial infection. Lesions occurring on the face regularly cause deformities of the ears, mouth, and nose. This disease readily invades the body, causing severe bone pain, scarring, and deformities of the skeleton. It is easy to detect yaws damage in ancient human skeletons. Unlike bejel, yaws does not attack the heart or nervous system. The infection is likely to occur during childhood when it is acquired by continuous contact with afflicted individuals. In some regions, the disease is found in 90 percent of the population, indicating that it is moderately contagious.

Syphilis, caused by *T. pallidum pallidum,* is the most common and widespread of the *Treponema* diseases. Like its sister diseases, syphilis starts out as a skin ailment, also producing a lesion where the organism entered the body. This lesion, called a chancre, eventually disappears as the bacterium spreads throughout the body. At this point in the disease, many people are fooled into thinking it has gone away. Next, a rash appears, accompanied by a feeling of being ill. The disease seems to disappear again, though, as the organism becomes further established in the body. Syphilis causes the most internal damage of the *Treponema* diseases. It causes destruction of many internal organs, doing extreme damage to the brain. Significant bone scarring and deformation, including the skull, characterize syphilis. Throughout the course of the disease it usually can be spread through sexual contact. Thus, it gets the name **venereal** disease, meaning that it is transmitted by sexual contact. The disease transfers to infants through the placenta or during childbirth, causing a condition called congenital syphilis.

Both domesticated and wild animals also suffer from *Treponema* diseases. Cattle develop a skin disease from *T. brennaborense. T. hydosenteriae* causes a stomach ailment in pigs. *Treponema* bacteria are commonly found in the digestive systems of cows, pigs, and sheep. *Treponemas* usually do not cause disease in animals, however. Rather, they assist other microorganisms with the breakdown of foods. Even insects such as termites are now known to have beneficial *Treponemas* that aid digestion. It is believed cockroaches also carry these bacteria. *T. azotonutricium* is an unusual type that helps termites, and likely other animals, obtain nitrogen from their foods. It gives animals the ability to use food the same way a plant uses fertilizer to obtain nutrients. Normally, animals can only obtain nitrogen in the form of protein.

ORIGINS AND EVOLUTION OF HUMAN DISEASES

Biologists have strong evidence that most human diseases started out from **parasites** or ailments in other animals. Parasites are organisms that live off of the bodily resources of a host. Although parasites are harmful to the host, they generally will not kill it, as the host provides the parasite with the resources it needs to survive. Many internal parasites remain throughout the life of the host. Pathogens are organisms that cause diseases in others. Their presence somehow alters the host's body, causing illness or death. A pathogen's survival is based on the fact that it will reproduce or successfully transfer to another host before the original host dies. Parasites are thought to be former pathogens that have had long contact with their host. Organisms that cannot adapt to the invasion of pathogens ultimately die off. Pathogens that are too aggressive will also die off if they wipe out all their hosts. Therefore, over many generations a balancing process takes place that converts pathogens to parasites. Interactions between the genetic mutations of the pathogen and the host lead to this harmony.

How does one animal acquire the parasites or diseases of another? First, there needs to be proximity between the animals. The two animals must share a similar space so they can have enough contact for the disease to spread. Human settlement in wilderness areas is one way that brings people into regular contact with animals. It is known that the bubonic plague, also known as the Black Death, and hanta-

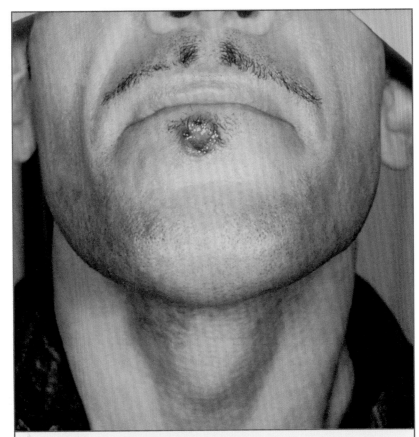

Figure 4.3 During the early stages of the disease, syphilis causes chancres (like the one on this man's chin), which form around the area where it entered the body. Chancres usually disappear as syphilis spreads throughout the body and moves toward the secondary stage. (Centers for Disease Control and Prevention)

virus, which produces a type of hemorrhagic fever, are both acquired from rodents. The disease-producing organisms made their way into humans as rodents were forced to live among humans. The rodents remained around the human dwellings as they lost their habitat and access to food. This greatly increased the chance that the rodent diseases would make contact with humans.

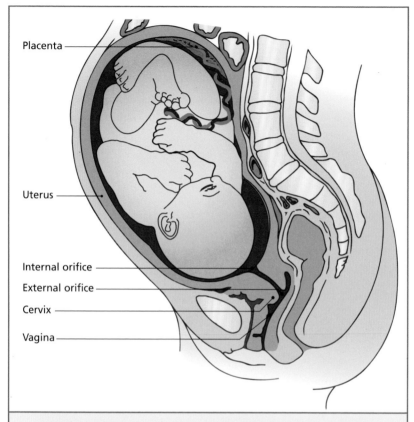

Placenta

Uterus

Internal orifice

External orifice

Cervix

Vagina

Figure 4.4 Syphilis can be passed from a mother to her unborn child through the placenta. Congenital syphilis can lead to birth defects including deformities and organ failure.

Sometimes contact with an animal does not have to be direct to pick up another animal's diseases. Blood-sucking insects typically spread a variety of diseases within a population of animals and even plants. Fleas carry bubonic plague from one rat to another. Lyme disease and Rocky Mountain spotted fever are spread among grazing animals by ticks. Malaria, one of the most devastating diseases in the world, is transmitted through the bite of the *Anopheles* mosquito. As animals come into proximity with other animals, it is expected that any biting pests will be shared. This sharing becomes the means of transferring parasites and pathogens among the different species.

Pathogen contact alone does not produce a disease. The new host must provide a good environment for the invading pathogen. Mutations normally found in a population of pathogens make each one more likely to survive in specific animals. Regular contact between different animals increases the chance that a mutant form will find a new host that it can successfully invade. Influenza viruses, which cause flu, show a high rate of mutation and easily transfer from one type of host to another. Recently, this has been noted with West Nile virus, a disease

Figure 4.5 Cows on a farm share close quarters and aid the spread of communicable diseases. Animals that share small habitats, such as farms or zoos, are more at risk of catching certain diseases, and contact with people can spread diseases to the human population. The smallpox virus, for example, is believed to have originated from human contact with animals infected with the related cowpox virus. (U.S. Department of Agriculture)

that is fatal in birds and causes a type of meningitis in mammals. Researchers are confirming that subtle mutations in the virus permitted the spread of the disease from birds to humans. The common form, or wild type, found in birds does not cause significant problems in humans.

The domestication of animals and the formation of huge urban areas is now known to be a major reason for the abundance and great diversity of human diseases. Few diseases were recorded by ancient civilizations. It is believed that this was not due to a lack of diagnosis but rather to an absence of disease. Close contact with domesticated animals provided the opportunity for many animal diseases to spread throughout the human population. The common ailment of children called conjunctivitis or pinkeye is identical to a contagious eye disease of cattle. Similarly, the notorious smallpox virus, feared for its use in biological warfare, is closely related to the cowpox virus of cattle. Domesticated cattle date back almost 10,000 years. This long relationship with cattle also gave us measles and tuberculosis. Likewise, the domestication of pigs introduced humans to flu and pertussis.

Urbanization increased the spread of animal diseases among humans. First, the housing found in early urban areas provided a favorable environment for disease spreading among family members. Many bacteria and viruses were safe in the stagnant and dark environments of early dwellings. Therefore, any organisms remaining on beds, tables, and other surfaces survived outside of the body longer than they would out in the open. The high density of people living in cities increased the chances that the new diseases would successfully move from one human host to another. In effect, humans created their diseases as civilization expanded from tribal settlements to major metropolitan regions.

The best-studied contemporary example of a disease being transmitted from animals to humans is AIDS, caused by the human immunodeficiency virus (HIV). Viruses related to HIV are found in a variety of animals, including common domesticated ones such as cats and horses. It is now accepted that humans picked up the AIDS virus, HIV 3, from apes carrying a related virus called the simian immunodeficiency virus (SIV). The virus produces cancer-type diseases in the primate carriers. HIV 3 just happens to cause a variation of disease that leads to AIDS rather than to cancer. Researchers continue to debate the period when the HIV mutation appeared. Japanese researchers argue that HIV came about around 300 years ago. Jonas Salk, discoverer of the polio vaccine, contended that the virus jumped from apes to humans about 900 years ago. How the disease passed from apes to humans is hotly disputed. No matter when the mutation occurred and how the virus spread to humans, its impact on humans has been devastating.

The origin of syphilis may also be related to contact with animals harboring *Treponema* and related spirochetes. Some ancient animal skeletons gave faint evidence of *Treponema* in mammals other than humans. However, the spirochete bone scarring cannot be confirmed as coming from *Treponema*. The recent discovery of a novel strain of *Treponema* called *T. brennaborense* in dairy cows provides a direct link to how it may have first afflicted early humans. In cattle, this organism causes an ulcer-producing disease called digital dermatitis. Early humans may have contracted *Treponema* by handling the flesh of wild cattle and related grazing animals. Cattle also carry *T. bryantii*, a beneficial bacterium that helps with the digestive breakdown of plants. It is probably unrelated to the types of *Treponema* that cause human disease. Rabbits also carry a pathogenic *Treponema* called *T. cuniculi*. This type produces a condition called rabbit syphilis, which closely resembling syphilis in humans. This also may have been the source of human syphilis.

Most biologists agree that *T. carateum* and *T. pallidum* came from some common ancestor more than 1.5 million years ago. Too little is known about the evolution of *T. amy-*

lovorum to reach any conclusions about its relationship to syphilis. Evidence about the origins of syphilis was uncovered in a study showing *Treponema* scarring in 500,000-year-old *Homo erectus* bones from southern Italy. It is assumed that the scarring was caused by *T. carateum*. This indicates that *Treponema* has had a long association with humans. *T. carateum* probably spread through ancient humans as pinta, unchanged over the 500,000 years. However, it is very difficult to trace the history and incidence of pinta because it rarely causes bone scarring. More is known about the different varieties of *T. pallidum*. Again, there are no studies investigating the presence of *T. amylovorum* in ancient human skeletons or old dental specimens.

A comparison of bejel, yaws, and syphilis gives a fairly accurate depiction of how syphilis came about. Bejel, from *T. pallidum endemicum*, and yaws, from *T. pallidum pertenue*, produce a superficial skin infection that minimally invades internal organs. These two diseases have been confirmed in ancient skeletons collected around the world. Yaws was confirmed on bones collected from the Mariana Islands, in the Pacific Ocean, dated A.D. 850. Inhabitants of these islands could not have picked up the disease from the new location. They had to bring it there. So it appears that the disease hitchhiked with early humans as they left Africa for Asia, Europe, North America, and various islands scattered around the oceans.

There is no evidence that syphilis infected ancient people. Mummified remains of humans show none of the damage associated with *T. pallidum*. Plus, no accurately documented records of syphilis were found until the disease started showing up commonly in Europe during the 1500s. The severity of the disease indicates that it may have developed from a more dangerous type of bejel or yaws that readily invaded the body. Some interesting data show that syphilis was introduced after bejel and yaws. In regions with both bejel and syphilis, the syphilis only shows up in urban

THE PSYCHOLOGY OF SYPHILIS

Fears are a normal part of the human experience. Many fears have legitimate origins, such as the ancient dread of being bitten by snakes or the modern fear of flying in airplanes. Both have a risk that can be life threatening. Certain snakebites can be poisonous and airplanes can malfunction. Fear abounded in Europe as diseases spread unrelentingly throughout the population. Bubonic plague, cholera, and leprosy were worthy of fear. They were incurable diseases that traveled with stealth from one community to another. The conditions were usually severe and in most cases resulted in a horrible death. People took any precaution possible to avoid contracting these diseases. The outbreak of syphilis caused unequalled concern. It was a new disease with no definite cause or remedies. The disease also remained hidden in some people, making it almost impossible to predict who should be avoided and who should be quarantined. Fears are acceptable in society as long as they do not turn into phobias.

A phobia is an extreme reaction to a fear. People with phobias feel undue stress that can lead to severe restrictions in the person's lifestyle. For example, people with agoraphobia, the fear of large spaces, have trouble leaving their houses because they want to avoid the expansive outdoors. Syphilophobia, a dread fear of syphilis, ran throughout eighteenth- and nineteenth-century Europe and Asia as the disease spread. This condition, recognized as a legitimate psychological disorder, drove people to avoid any action that might cause syphilis. Some people avoided even the casual touch of others. In more recent years, toilet seats, locker rooms, and money became the targets of disease spread for syphilophobics. Syphilophobia struck the British royal family in the seventeenth century when it was requested that King Charles II use condoms to avoid the disease. In American history, the condition affected whole communities, leading to campaigns to eradicate illicit sexual activities. Chicago was the largest city to express syphilophobia. The city implemented a highly controversial War on Syphilis campaign that lasted from 1937 to 1940.

areas of the region, where bejel is not common. People living in regions having yaws only get syphilis when yaws is eradicated through public health programs. Bejel and yaws provide immunity from syphilis; therefore a person having one of those diseases is unlikely to contract syphilis. Syphilis did not establish a stronghold in these regions because the pre-existing treponemal diseases, bejel and yaws, restricted its spread. Also, *T. pallidum's* role as a pathogen rather than as a benign parasite probably means that it has not had the time to evolve a harmonious relationship with humans. Although some changes have come to the disease, it is a much milder disease today than when it first ravaged Europe in the 1600s.

The types of mutations turning *Treponema* into the sexually transmitted disease syphilis are not known. It is thought that these mutations arose in the New World about 1,600 years ago, well before Christopher Columbus's visit. However, scientists agree that the change from a contact disease of youth to a sexually transmitted disease was beneficial for the survival *Treponema*. Young people with bejel and yaws are likely to die before reproductive age or are less likely to have children as a result of the disease. This obviously reduces the spread of the pathogen. Spread by sexual contact, on the other hand, protects younger individuals and ensures the organism will be passed on to previously healthy adults. Its spread around the world was also facilitated by travelers transmitting it through repeated sexual contacts with native inhabitants.

5

Prevention and Treatment of Syphilis

Marion County, Indiana, public health officials were startled by a dramatic increase in syphilis cases during the first three months of 2008. By August of that year, they had identified 89 cases, which was the highest number the county had seen in seven years. Indianapolis, the largest city in Marion County, had most of the cases. The number of cases exceeded all of the syphilis cases diagnosed in 2007. This surprised health department officials because the number of syphilis cases in Indianapolis was generally much lower than equivalent cities in other states. There was no explanation given for the explosion in syphilis cases. However, health officials are seeking ways, such as public awareness programs, to curb the spread of syphilis.[1]

American diplomat and scientist Benjamin Franklin commented in *Poor Richard's Almanac,* "He's the best physician that knows the worthlessness of the most medicines." He observed the unusual and dangerous strategies used with little success to treat a variety of ailments plaguing society. Treatments that would be considered quackery today, such as **bloodletting** and the breathing of "healing" fragrances, dominated medical practices.

Syphilis, "the Great Imitator," created many problems when it was first recognized in Europe as a distinct disease. Little was known about identifying and treating the disease. At first it was confused as another form of other diseases such as anthrax, black plague, leprosy, and smallpox. Therefore either it was treated inappropriately or not treated at all because it was considered incurable. An additional problem about syphilis was that nobody knew for sure what caused it and how it spread. Early cures and preventative measures had little value because they were founded on metaphysical principles rather than medical evidence. A third problem with trying to control syphilis was the newness of the disease. It was a modern disease with no traditional treatments in the ancient Greek, Hebrew, or Roman herbals and medical writings. Even the Arabic and Asian healing arts entering Europe bit by bit provided no options for eradicating syphilis.

EARLY VIEWS OF THERAPY

At the onset of syphilis in the late 1400s, the severity and appalling nature of the disease restricted medical analysis. Physicians were afraid to visit syphilis patients and refused to touch them. Most physicians rejected all syphilis patients because they were afraid of contracting the disease. They saw how the body quickly developed "acorn-sized boils that emitted a foul, dark green pus," as described by German knight Ulrich von Hutten in his popular book about syphilis, published in the early 1500s. Even Girolamo Fracastoro, the Italian physician who unwittingly gave syphilis its name, viewed it as a terribly fatal disease accompanied by "ulcers that dissolved the skin, muscle, bone, palate, and tonsils." His description of the disease was intended to induce fear in an attempt to control its spread throughout Europe. Imagine what it was like to read about an incurable disease with symptoms such as "violent pains tormenting the afflicted, who were exhausted but could not sleep, suffered starvation without feeling hungry." No wonder physicians wanted nothing to do with syphilis patients.

Initially, syphilis patients were not treated mostly because of the philosophy of physicians such as M. Flamand of France, who believed that venereal diseases were the "just rewards of unbridled lust." The sin of sex, and not the actual intercourse,

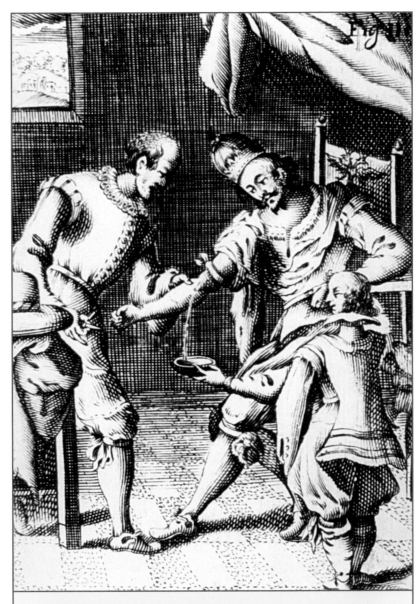

Figure 5.1 People once believed that syphilis was caused by an accumulation of bad humors (fluids) in the body and that removing those humors would restore the patient's health. As such, bloodletting was a common practice. (National Library of Medicine)

was thought to spread the condition. Therefore, syphilis was justifiably imposed by God as punishment for sin. Physicians questioned if it was wise to go against the wisdom of God by easing the affliction. This analysis added to the tacit refusal of physicians to treat syphilis, some of whom went so far as to cast patients into the streets.

Any treatments applied to syphilis in Europe from the 1400s through the 1500s were founded on local cultural and religious beliefs. Sin was considered the foremost cause of diseases in humans as well as in domesticated animals and plants. Dirty habits around the house, a sin in those times, created infestations of lice, fleas, and roaches. Other sins, such as an unclean mind, were thought to lead to different degrees of ailments ranging from common colds to black plague, determined by the severity of sinning. So the horrible sin of illicit sex obviously was punished with the equally terrible affliction of syphilis. Encounters with "lawless" people and "barbarians" were also viewed as actions that created disease. This perspective eliminated the idea that local citizens were involved in heinous sins. The problem was more of an invasion by sin.

Diseases of sins were treated according to the various cures developed in Europe during the Roman influence of Europe, starting about 200 B.C., and ending about A.D. 900, after the reign of Charlemagne. These therapies were then modified by Christian clerics during the Dark Ages. Treatments were made applicable to the sins creating the ailments. New views of medicine were heralded during the 1200s and 1400s through various developments: the growth of scholasticism in European universities, the introduction of Middle Eastern philosophy during the Crusades, and the influence of Asian therapies brought in by trade.

Metaphysical syphilis therapies prevailed during the early outbreak of this STD scourge. They included customized prayers by the afflicted, incantations by clerics, amulets or religious symbols worn by the afflicted, and **herbal remedies** similar to aromatherapy. Some physicians took a blended meta-

SYPHILIS: A Rationale for Various Treatments

Each culture's interpretation of syphilis determined the type of preventative methods and cures that were used. Today, most people in the world readily accept that syphilis is caused by a bacterium and can be treated with antibiotics. However, little if anything was known about the cause of syphilis when it first materialized in Europe. Efforts to control the disease were based on previous experience with other disorders. At first, common poisons believed to have purifying effects on the body were used as treatments. Pure metals such as gold and mercury served that role. These remedies had little effect, but that did not stop people from believing in their use. The common ideology was that a person would be worse off without the therapy. A known toxin called Salvarsan, or arsphenamine, which contains arsenic, was even promoted by noted scientists, including Paul Erhlich who won a Nobel Prize for his work on disease treatment.

Other purifying methods such as bloodletting and herbal medicines followed. Some herbal therapies are still used today to ward off syphilis. Many homeopathic practitioners prescribe herbs that interact with the syphilitic psyche. For example, syphilis makes a person feel desperate, destructive, and hopeless. Thus, treatments that bring people out of those states of mental anguish help alleviate syphilis. Probably the most obscure use of herbs in treating syphilis involves a common salad component. During the Middle Ages carrots were thought to relieve the body of syphilis and other ailments. The vegetable made its way to Europe from Afghanistan in the tenth century by trade under the Byzantine Empire.

physical and medical approach by administering herbal potions intended to flush disease and sin from the body. Skin disorders associated with syphilis were likely treated with chicken broth and saliva. It was thought that chicken broth and saliva had magical powers that rid the body of demons, serpents, and worms derived from sinful acts. The use of poisonous metals and salts was also common in treating a variety of diseases. Gold, mercury, and silver were ingested or introduced into the patient's blood as a means of purifying the body. By accident, these metals sometimes had some benefits because they killed the microorganisms and reduced damage caused by the immune system.

Bloodletting and **leeching** were probably also applied to syphilis during its early outbreaks. The practice of draining blood is based on the principle that blood contains the humors controlling the body's health, and an accumulation of bad humors in the blood produces disease. Blood was drained from the body using surgical instruments or leeches. Sometimes bloodletting led directly to death from extreme and rapid blood loss. However, the calming effects of bloodletting, attributable to a weakened state created by blood loss, were measured as successful treatment. Related treatments included drilling holes in the skull to prevent or relieve mental afflictions. Other medical treatments included cauterizing syphilis sores with a hot iron to sterilize and seal the wounds.

By the 1600s it was well established that the act of sex spread something that caused syphilis. This insight, plus the growing desperation to combat the swift spread of syphilis, coerced hospitals and physicians to seek rational ways of stemming the tide of the disease. Regulations against fornication led the prevention methods. It was believed that syphilis was spread by sex with "inferior" and "base" individuals. Prostitutes with syphilis who did not stop their practices were banished, branded, and sometimes killed. Dutch scholar Desiderius Erasmus (1496–1536) went as far as proposing the binding and castration of women with syphilis. The immigration of syphilitics was also restricted in order to reduce its spread in a country or region. Hospitals treated syphilitic people with leprosy and tuberculosis by placing them in quarantine clinics.

THE ROAD TO TREATING SYPHILIS

The discovery of *T. pallidum pallidum* as the cause of syphilis opened the door for rational preventive methods and cures. *T. pallidum pallidum* was difficult to link to syphilis because of its elusive nature. Like many spirochetes, *T. pallidum pallidum* is difficult to isolate in the laboratory. It does not survive under the conditions traditionally used to maintain disease-causing microorganisms. Therefore researchers were not able to grow *T. pallidum pallidum* from wounds and tissues of syphilitic patients. Unfortunately, this method is an important step in the identification of microbial diseases. In the 1870s, German physician Robert Koch developed specific criteria for determining the cause of a disease, known as Koch's postulates (Table 5.1). Another factor confounding the discovery of *T. pallidum pallidum* was that it did not cause actual syphilis in traditional laboratory animals used by early

TABLE 5.1   KOCH'S POSTULATES

1. The specific organism should be shown to be present in all cases of animals suffering from a specific disease but should not be found in healthy animals.

2. The specific microorganism should be isolated from the diseased animal and grown in pure culture on artificial laboratory media.

3. This freshly isolated microorganism, when inoculated into a healthy laboratory animal, should cause the same disease seen in the original animal.

4. The microorganism should be reisolated in pure culture from the experimental infection.

Figure 5.2 Russian scientist Elie Metchnikoff, pictured here in his laboratory, discovered that *T. pallidum pallidum* caused syphilis. (Library of Congress)

scientists. It could only be studied on human subjects, which is also true for AIDS today.

The meticulous work of Russian scientist Elie Metchnikoff, with the assistance of French scientist Pierre Roux, set the stage for the discovery and treatment of *T. pallidum pallidum* as the cause of syphilis. In 1903 the two scientists successfully transferred the then unknown organism from humans to chimpanzees. *T. pallidum pallidum* survived in the chimpanzees and caused lesions similar to those of humans suffering from syphilis. The two scientists were also able to transmit syphilis between chimpanzees using the same technique of inoculating the chimpanzees with infected tissue. Metchnikoff and Roux also learned that inoculation with small amounts of the organism provided slight resistance at the time of subsequent exposure. This was proved many years later with the observations that exposure to bejel and yaws reduces the chance of contracting syphilis. Italian scientists were later able to induce syphilis-like sores on the scrotums of rabbits using a similar technique.

It was not until 1905 that *T. pallidum pallidum* made its appearance under the microscope. Fritz Schaudinn and Erich Hoffman isolated the spirochete from chancres on people confirmed to have syphilis. Normal microscopic analysis would not have shown *T. pallidum pallidum*. They had to use techniques reserved for bloodborne parasites and pathogens developed by hematologists (blood specialists). Scientists were now ready to precisely combat the disease, knowing that syphilis was caused by a bacterium. However, adequate syphilis therapy was not available until drugs called **antibiotics** were discovered.

Antibiotic therapy would not have been discovered if not for a fortuitous observation by Alexander Fleming in 1929 (Figure 5.3). He discovered that the fungus *Penicillium* produced a secretion that kills bacteria in laboratory cultures. The secretion turned out to be the antibiotic penicillin. Fleming and other researchers turned this observation into a possible therapy for treating bacterial diseases. By 1940, English scientists Howard Florey and Ernst Chain confirmed the effectiveness of penicillin in killing bacteria in animal and human trials. Its greatest use came during World War II to treat a variety of bacterial infections of wounds. Now there

Figure 5.3 Penicillin, a widely used antibiotic today, was discovered in 1929 by Alexander Fleming. Fleming is shown here at work in his laboratory. (© AP Images)

was hope for controlling the unrelenting spread of other bacterial diseases such as syphilis.

MODERN SYPHILIS THERAPY

The first step in ridding the world of syphilis involved the use of antibiotics. Initial successes curing other bacterial diseases justified their use for treating syphilis. Fleming's penicillin became the choice treatment for syphilis during

World War II. Its effectiveness during the war translated into its regular use throughout the world. Penicillin injections into muscle proved effective against the primary and secondary stages of syphilis. It killed *T. pallidum pallidum* immediately, preventing it from spreading throughout the body and advancing the disease. Latent and tertiary syphilis are not as simple to treat as the earlier stages. They require long-term penicillin treatments to catch the bacteria at a time when they are normally vulnerable to antibiotic treatments. Penicillin is most effective when bacteria are reproducing rapidly. *T. pallidum pallidum* is not involved in much growth during the latent and tertiary stages.

Antibiotic treatments proved to be the most valuable strategy for eliminating syphilis from the body. In 2009, the Centers for Disease Control and Prevention in Atlanta, Georgia, continued recommending the original type of penicillin called **penicillin G** as the primary treatment for new cases of syphilis. A single dose at 2.4 million units injected into the muscles is found to work well for primary and secondary syphilis.

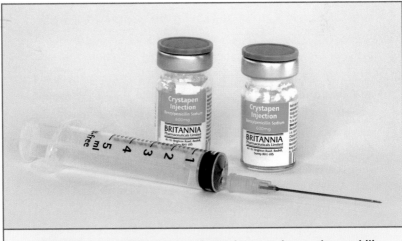

Figure 5.4 Penicillin works against primary and secondary syphilis. It is usually administered via an injection to a large muscle group (upper arm or thigh). (© Kumar Sriskandan/Alamy)

This therapy is also recommended for treating syphilis in pregnant women because penicillin is not known to harm the fetus. Latent and tertiary syphilis must be treated with a total of 7.2 million units of penicillin G, also injected into the muscle, over a period of three weekly doses. Neurosyphilis—central nervous system involvement resulting from a long-term syphilis infection—is treated with intravenous penicillin G treatments for at least two weeks. Similar treatment regimens prove effective against other *T. pallidum* diseases such as bejel and yaws.

Unfortunately for many people, the penicillin treatments given for syphilis can cause an intense fever called the **Jarisch-Herxheimer reaction**. This condition develops within two days after treatment and may lead to headaches and muscle pain. Fever-reducing drugs are usually given at the first signs of Jarisch-Herxheimer. Metchnikoff's original studies focused on controlling syphilis sores with topical applications to the chancres. So far, no effective oral or topical penicillin therapies exist. If given early in the infection, during early or even latent disease, the patient will be cured and without any permanent damage. Sadly, the antibiotic treatments for syphilis do not undo any damage caused by the bacteria; the bone decay, skin scarring, and any organ damage remain. Luckily, the body may slowly heal some of the damage, assuming the person is healthy and remains free of other infectious diseases.

Many people suffer from antibiotic allergies. Penicillin in particular cause dangerous allergic reactions that at their mildest lead to fever and hives. At its worst, penicillin can induce the cessation of breathing during what is termed an anaphylactic reaction. Therefore, other antibiotics may have to be administered instead to prevent harm to the patient during syphilis treatment. Doxycycline and tetracycline are commonly recommended for patients with penicillin allergies. The treatment regime is different than that for penicillin. First, both of these drugs must be taken orally, possibly reducing their effectiveness if they are not taken properly. Doxycycline is taken in 100-mg doses twice a day for 14 days. Tetracycline must be administered in 500-mg amounts four times a day for 14 days.

The unfortunate overuse of antibiotics in Europe and North America has lead to the production of antibiotic-resistant bacteria called "superbugs." Superbugs are micro-organisms unaffected by common drug therapies. Genetic mutations in the bacteria protect them from the antibiotics. These mutations are encouraged when antibiotics are over-used or not administered properly. The United Kingdom's House of Lords Select Committee on Science and Technology best acknowledged the severity of the superbug problem in a 1998 report. It stated: "This enquiry [into antibiotic resis-tance] has been an alarming experience, which leaves us con-vinced that resistance to antibiotics and other anti-infective agents constitutes a major threat to public health and ought to be recognised as such much more widely than it is at present." The report made medical officials aware that the uncontrolled spread of superbugs can cause public health to regress to the days before antibiotics.

Fortunately, to date, penicillin resistance has not emerged in *T. pallidum pallidum*. Efforts to find oral alter-natives, such as azithromycin, have run into problems with resistance developing. In countries with limited resources, arranging intravenous or intramuscular medications can be challenging. Other antibiotic treatments must be devel-oped. This is not such an easy task because not all antibiotics are effective at controlling *T. pallidum pallidum*. The ultimate nightmare is the appearance of bacteria resistant to all known antibiotics. Developing nations are at a severe dis-advantage when they encounter multiple antibiotic-resistant bacteria because they have little or no access to expensive alter-native therapies.

Probably the best way to control syphilis is to control its spread. Early detection of syphilis is most important in prevent-ing the spread from person to person. It also limits the degree of damage caused to the body if detected early. In 1906, a means of detecting syphilis was developed by Dr. August von Wassermann. His test, called the Wassermann test, uses antibodies to find *Treponema* in blood and tissue samples taken from people suspected of having syphilis. Modern variations of the Wassermann test are used today. These new tests, called **immunoassays**, are better able to find small amounts of bacteria in the body. A particularly sensitive test, called the *T. pallidum* **hemagglutination assay (TPHA)**, uses antibodies to clump red blood cells when syphilis is present in a sample.

The use of condoms designed for STD reduction greatly decreases the chance of contracting syphilis during sexual contact. Most condoms are effective and if properly used. Old and torn condoms are ineffective, as are condoms used with lubricants that decay the protective material. Other birth control devices are not effective in preventing the spread of syphilis. Certain public health agencies and schools encourage teaching young people abstinence from sexual contact as an effective way of reducing STDs such as syphilis. While abstinence from sexual activity drastically reduces one's exposure to STDs, these diseases also are preventable by following safer-sex practices (such as using condoms during sexual contact) or limiting the number of sexual partners and restricting sex to **monogamous** relationships (in which both partners have been tested for the presence of STDs). People whose sex education consists only of learning abstinence but not these safer-sex practices are vulnerable to exposing themselves to STDs if they one day decide to engage in sexual activities.

The recent growth of **homeopathy** and natural medicine is producing a demand for alternative medical treatments for syphilis. Many of these treatments date back to the Roman and Greek herbal remedies used around 400 B.C. Their purported effectiveness is not based on medical experimentation or study. So, physicians and scientists highly doubt that the treatments work. Herbal treatments for controlling or preventing syphilis include the use of tropical trees, such as lignum vitae sap applied to sores and lignum sanctum bark given as a broth. Dried earthworms used as lignum treatments eventually proved ineffective. An old treatment using ingested almond oil is still used today. Other traditional herbal therapies for syphilis commonly recommended today include extracts or leaves of plants related to blueberries, daisies, lilies, lobelias, mustards, and tomatoes. A new candidate is a cure-all plant from India called neem. Neem produces an oil that purportedly cures syphilis when used as a sexual lubricant. None of these folk remedies has been tested and none should be assumed to work.

6

Epidemiology of Syphilis

In March 2008, U.S. News and World Report *reported that the syphilis rate had grown for the seventh year in row. In a 2005 study, the Centers for Disease Control and Prevention (CDC) determined that the increase was mostly in gay and bisexual males. They feared that this was due to a lack of proper safer-sex precautions for reducing the spread of sexually transmitted diseases. The CDC is working with physicians to better monitor sexually transmitted diseases in this population. Some researchers debate the conclusions of the CDC study. The study also concluded that rises in syphilis, and many other diseases, are natural cycles and should not cause alarm.[1]*

Investigators who study the science of epidemiology exercise a type of skepticism expressed in the Latin proverb "Believe nothing and be on your guard against anything." Many think that it is a simple task to determine how diseases spread. However, the opposite is true, even given the abundance of current medical technology. This difficulty is readily evident in the media's reporting of medical findings. Researchers are regularly reported as disputing the causes of widespread maladies such as cancer and heart disease. Even the causes and spread of infectious diseases were subjects of heated debates until more was learned through rigorous investigation and fortuitous findings. Little was known about the cause, diagnosis, and spread of AIDS until many years after its first recognized appearance.

People and physicians had no systematic means of analyzing the spread of disease in the 1400s during the first syphilis outbreak in Europe. They blamed the scourge on a variety of factors, usually related to a breach of cultural values or a plague acquired from undesirable people. The disease spread worldwide because of ignorance about its

Figure 6.1 We now know how important it is to wash your hands after you sneeze to prevent the transmission of germs. Scientists did not always understand how diseases were passed from person to person. Hungarian physician Ignaz Semmelweis, shown here, provided an understanding of infectious disease transmission. (National Library of Medicine)

diagnosis and transmission. It was not until the 1840s that people obtained a firm grasp of applying scientifically sound rationales to understanding the spread of infectious diseases. Hungarian physician Ignaz Semmelweis set the foundations for epidemiology methods while investigating the spread of puerperal fever in maternity wards. His astute observations traced the spread of the bacterial disease to improper hand washing and sanitary practices by physicians. Unfortunately, Semmelweis's contemporaries were not willing to accept his findings and failed to exercise his precautions for reducing the spread of bacteria. It did not become a recommended practice until a short time after Semmelweis's death. To this day, though, physicians strictly apply the cleanliness practices (sterile techniques in today's language) promoted by Semmelweis.

Epidemiological studies have taught scientists much about the causes of the initial onset of syphilis in fifteenth-century Europe. Epidemiology also explains syphilis's persistent global presence today. With this knowledge, public health officials can reduce the impact of the disease and prevent a repeat of the horrible outbreaks that took place throughout Europe and European-settled lands between the late 1400s and early 1900s. Understanding the epidemiology of syphilis requires knowledge of its diagnosis and transmission. A disease cannot be adequately studied if it is difficult to detect in infected individuals. In addition, knowledge of how syphilis spreads from one person to another is needed to develop strategies for preventing its uncontrolled proliferation.

DIAGNOSING SYPHILIS

Determining whether a person has an infectious disease involves two critical observations: (1) recognizing characteristic signs and symptoms of the disease, and (2) confirming the presence of the disease by isolating and identifying the organism causing that ailment. Syphilis was at first difficult to diagnose because its victims manifested signs and symptoms similar to other common disorders. In addition, the body shows little evidence of the disease until about three weeks after infection. Unlike a cold or flu, syphilis does not hit all at once. This makes it difficult to tell when and from whom the disease was contracted. Today, the characteristic diagnostic features of syphilis are chancres at predictable

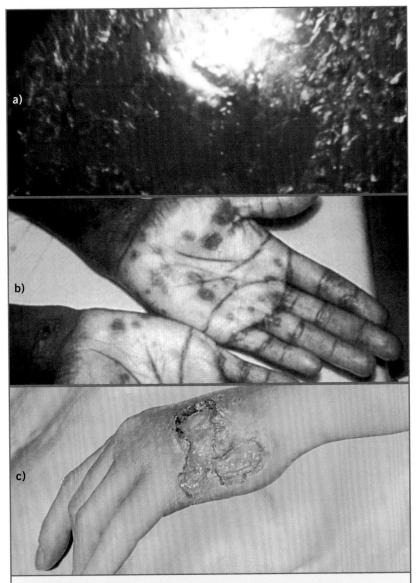

Figure 6.2 The three stages of syphilis: (a) primary syphilis is defined by the presence of chancres at the site of infection; (b) a patient with secondary syphilis develops a spotty rash; (c) tertiary syphilis results in the formations of gummas on the surface of the skin as well as internally. (Susan Lindsley/CDC/U.S. Department of Health and Human Services)

parts of the body that could become infected. Chancres that resemble other diseases can be confirmed as being caused by *T. pallidum pallidum* using medical tests such as the Wassermann test. Since syphilis is an STD, chancres are predominantly found around the genitals, but can be found around the mouth as well. Lesions on mucous membranes, a spotting skin rash usually on the palms and soles of feet, and general aches and pains best identify secondary syphilis. Latent syphilis confounds diagnosis because it provides no easily observable signs or symptoms. Tertiary syphilis is best identified by linking the presence of gummas and other signs to the patient's disease history.

A meeting of dermatologists in 1889 established the first organized attempt at standardizing the identification of syphilis during routine medical diagnosis. French physician Henri Feulard summoned an international group of dermatologists to construct criteria for recognizing syphilis. They settled on the criteria described above with other evidence of immune system attack by spirochetes. Over the years the group established criteria for a host of other diseases that can be characterized by specific skin conditions. These criteria must be reviewed regularly because the disease characteristics may change throughout time, as has occurred with syphilis since it first appeared in Europe.

Identifying the signs and symptoms alone is not sufficient for confirming the presence of syphilis. Diagnostic tests indicating the presence of *T. pallidum pallidum*, and nothing else, substantiate that a patient has the disease. Patients suspected of having syphilis are first interviewed to assess their level of sexual activity. People who were actively engaged in sex two to four weeks prior to the suspected indications of primary syphilis are very likely to have the disease. It would be highly unusual for a patient to have the early stages of syphilis if he or she was not engaged in any type of sexual activity. Similar background can be gathered for observations pointing to secondary and tertiary syphilis. At this point physicians can speculate if the syphilis was congenital or acquired by sexual contact. Luckily, syphilis is not spread by casual encounters, contact with animals, or insect and tick bites. This restricts the search for how the disease suspected to be syphilis was probably acquired.

Elie Metchnikoff and Pierre Roux were the first to learn that the chancres and sores of syphilitic patients contained and transmitted the infectious agent now known as *T. pallidum pallidum*. In effect, they provided the basis for determining syphilis by seeing if the isolated organism caused similar lesions in chimpanzees. Unfortunately, this test was not suitable for quick treatment because it took at least two weeks for chimpanzees to show the signs of syphilis, if at all. Also, the test was very expensive, requiring the sacrifice of several chimpanzees for one patient. The same would be true if the test was performed on rabbits. Most important, Metchnikoff and Roux did not know the nature of the organism being transmitted. There was no proof that it was *T. pallidum pallidum*. It could have been another organism causing the disease. The presence of *T. pallidum pallidum* in the wounds, as determined by Fritz Schaudinn and Erich Hoffman, may have been purely coincidental.

Robert Koch's contributions to disease diagnosis removed the next hurdle for developing a way to positively identify *T. pallidum pallidum* in patients suspected of having syphilis. His postulates provided a guideline by which scientists could show that *T. pallidum pallidum* acting alone was indeed the cause of syphilis. The race began to find quick ways to confirm the presence of *T. pallidum pallidum* to attest that a patient was afflicted with syphilis. A breakthrough came in 1906, with the efforts of German microbiologist August von Wassermann, who developed a way to confirm the presence of *T. pallidum pallidum*. Wassermann found a way of confirming the presence of *T. pallidum pallidum* using information and strategies gathered from the new science of immunology. The test, now called the Wassermann reaction, begins with a sample of blood serum collected from the patient. The blood is then carefully mixed with dead or living *T. pallidum pallidum* obtained from pure laboratory cultures. Patients exposed to syphilis show a positive test when the immune system components in the blood immediately react to the bacterium. The serum of patients not infected with *T. pallidum pallidum* gives a negative test indicated by no reaction. A certain number of syphilis patients have negative test results, adding some inaccuracy to the test. Wassermann was also able to adapt the test as a way of telling whether syphilis had responded to treatment. Removal of *T. pallidum pallidum* from the body is confirmed by several negative Wassermann reactions over a period of a few years after treatment.

Over the years, the Wassermann reaction was gradually improved to increase its sensitivity and accuracy. It is now one of several tests used to confirm infection with *T. pallidum pallidum*. The latest modification of the Wasserman test is called the *T. pallidum* hemagglutination assay, abbreviated TPHA. TPHA detects patient antibodies that specifically attack *T. pallidum pallidum*. Most people produce defensive proteins called antibodies when microorganisms invade their bodies. White blood cells manufacture the antibodies for the purpose of binding to the attacking organism. The antibodies then serve as markers, labeling the bacteria for destruction and removal by various components of the immune system. Patients with *T. pallidum pallidum* antibodies show a clumping of red blood cells, or hemagglutination, in the serum. TPHA is useful for indicating all stages of syphilis but is most sensitive to primary and secondary syphilis. However, many public health officials are not satisfied with the TPHA because it is inherently not very sensitive. People with light or undeveloped infections of *T. pallidum pallidum* may have negative test results with this assay.

A new generation of syphilis testing may make it possible to detect the disease accurately long before the first signs are exhibited. In 2008, scientists at Johannes Gutenberg University in Germany modified a technique called **polymerase chain reaction** (PCR) to determine the presence of *T. pallidum pallidum* in skin samples. PCR uses minute amounts of DNA to identify the presence of a specific organism in a sample. The chemical reaction duplicates the DNA until a large enough sample can be collected for analysis. It is hoped that the test—which is much more sensitive than the Wasserman, TPHA, and other antibody methods—can be used on a variety of body samples including blood. This test is also more reliable than microscopic examinations of tissues in which the scientist must look for the *Treponema*. In addition, PCR can be used on old specimens to look for the origins of syphilis in human bodies dating back hundreds of years.

A more sensitive test is the Venereal Disease Research Laboratory test, known as the **VDRL** test. This test is commonly used to check for primary and secondary syphilis. VDRL also indicates the presence of *T. pallidum pallidum* antibodies in patient serum and tissue samples. Samples collected from suspect sores, blood, or spinal fluid are mixed with purified *T. pallidum pallidum* **antigens**. An easy-to-visualize reaction called flocculation occurs if the patient's blood has *T. pallidum pallidum* antibodies. The test is highly sensitive and can detect low levels of infection. Kit forms of the test are readily available to clinics and physicians and are sold as the rapid plasma reagin card test. Patient samples are placed on a small plastic card on which test results can be easily seen. However, the test is not accurate or effective for detecting the early onset of syphilis or syphilis that is in the last two stages.

Another way of detecting *T. pallidum pallidum* antibodies involves the use of **fluorescent** antibodies. The fluorescence, or bright glow, acts as a loud alarm announcing the presence of *T. pallidum pallidum* antibodies in serum and tissue samples. *T. pallidum pallidum* antibodies attached to fluorescent dyes are integrated into a test called the fluorescent treponemal antibody absorption test, or **FTA-ABS**. Samples containing *T. pallidum pallidum* antibodies give off a green glow when exposed to ultraviolet light. Fluorescent tests are much more sensitive than agglutination testing, which permits their use with all stages of syphilis. A related test uses proteins called enzymes to enhance the glow. These are called enzyme linked immunoabsorption assays, or **ELISA**. They are usually sold as simple kits that give immediate results.

The use of simple diagnostic kits for detecting syphilis in a doctor's office has created many problems for public health officials. Health workers administering the kits sometimes do not question the accuracy and precision of the testing. This oversight could possibly lead to misdiagnosis. Test kits are ineffective if they are not correctly used and handled. Kits require proper storage and must be used under the specific conditions stipulated by the manufacturer. Most governments prohibit the sale of syphilis test kits to the public because of the severe consequences of incorrect results. In January 2002, the Medical Devices Agency in England had to ban a syphilis ELISA kit because it was giving false data. The test regularly gave false-negative tests, meaning that people with syphilis were shown to be free of the disease. This created many legal problems when a pregnant woman using the test unknowingly passed along the disease to her child.

A 2006 report in Canada put a scare into the medical community. It found that none of the current syphilis tests respond to people with AIDS. The immune decay caused by the AIDS virus reduces the number of antibodies produced against syphilis and other diseases. In many cases the antibody number falls below what is needed for detection by the various tests described above. Neal denHollander, the Uni-

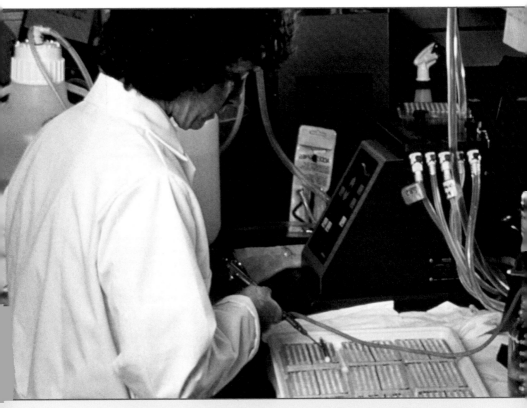

Figure 6.3 An ELISA, or enzyme linked immunoabsorption assay, is one way to test for syphilis. This test involves using a fluorescent tag to identify the presence of *T. pallidum pallidum* antibodies. (Centers for Disease Control and Prevention)

versity of Ontario microbiologist who led the study, sees a need for developing more effective ways of detecting syphilis in patients with immune systems weakened by ill health or infectious diseases. Despite these study results, most modern syphilis tests are effective in HIV-positive patients.

Diagnosing syphilis with clinical tests is only part of the syphilis control scenario. Public health agencies must try to trace the path of the particular infection that was just diagnosed and confirmed. Tracking the disease involves intensive interviews with the infected person. The person is obligated to report all the contacts that could have caused and further spread his or her case of syphilis. This may include admitting embarrassing personal details and may compromise the intimacy of certain relationships. Many married individuals found their marriages jeopardized when it was discovered that they had contracted syphilis through extramarital sex. All sexual partners must be notified to ensure that they are diagnosed and treated.

THE PREVALENCE OF SYPHILIS TODAY

One would think that syphilis would be a disease of the past considering all the marvelous medical and scientific advances for detecting and controlling *T. pallidum pallidum*. This belief is far from the truth. Epidemiologic studies worldwide show that syphilis is still common and widely transmitted in spite of many attempts to limit its spread. Syphilis still accounts for a majority of sexually transmitted diseases found throughout the world with 12 million confirmed cases reported in 2002. That means approximately 0.2 percent of the population, or 2 in 1,000 people, are known to have syphilis. In the United States, it was estimated in 2002 that 70,000 new cases of syphilis are detected annually. Some of these were repeat cases in prostitutes and sexually activity individuals. The rate of syphilis in the United States varies dramatically from year to year. Syphilis decreased from 1980 to 1997. Much of this was due to people taking greater precautions because of fear about AIDS. From 1997 to 2002, the number of new cases of syphilis increased. Canada has a much lower rate of syphilis than the United States. However, the rate of syphilis in Australia and the United Kingdom is exceeding the rate in the United States. The number of undiagnosed cases of syphilis worldwide is not known.

Research studies show that in developed nations syphilis is mostly spread by heterosexual sex in young adults. Young female drug addicts are currently the fastest-growing group contracting syphilis. It is believed that they acquire syphilis through sexual favors or prostitution performed to obtain the drugs. This has created a stark increase in the number of congenital syphilis cases. Male homosexuals account for another growing sector of syphilis patients. The improved control of the AIDS epidemic is making people less cautious about high-risk sexual behaviors. In addition, homosexuals are less likely than heterosexuals to use condoms. Condoms are considered an inconvenience by many people and are used almost exclusively to prevent pregnancy. Syphilis in developing nations is mostly a problem among prostitutes and people who are not educated about safe sex. Crowded urban areas have the highest incidence of STDs in these nations. However, the problem is compounded because few people seek treatment even if they know they are infected.

Syphilis today is most commonly found in association with other STDs. People with AIDS traditionally are candidates for a concurrent syphilis infection. Syphilis is more likely to spread unchecked when afflicted individuals have a weakened immune system, typically caused by AIDS. Chlamydial infection and gonorrhea also regularly accompany syphilis according to reports by the Centers for Disease Control. The number of STDs found in an individual is linked to the amount and frequency of his or her sexual contacts.

Although the incidence of syphilis is now lower than ever before in history, public health officials are fearful of the growing incidence of antibiotic-resistant infections. These bacteria are difficult to treat in developed nations and cannot be treated at all in developing nations. Public health officials already see an increase in other pathogenic multiple antibiotic-resistant bacteria such as the *Mycobacterium* that causes tuberculo-

A SYPHILIS VACCINE?

Public health officials are well aware that the best way to control disease is by preventing it. Treating the disease with medication does not necessarily remove the disease. Many diseases have become resistant to current drug treatments and withstand the best efforts to eradicate them. Syphilis is no exception. Although syphilis can be cured, the disease is best contained by preventing it from spreading throughout the population. This way, syphilis may ultimately disappear quickly or become so infrequent that the remaining cases can be eradicated after a while. Early campaigns to rid society of syphilis did not work because of unrealistic expectations. The government tried unsuccessfully to control people's sexual habits, thinking that strict codes against illicit sex and prostitution would be sufficient. However, people ignored and protested these regulations as they did drinking restrictions during Prohibition. In 2002, San Francisco, California, implemented the latest effort by a city to try imposing limitations on sexual behavior to curb the spread of STDs. The city started a public ad campaign in the schools advocating abstinence. As expected, it was unrealistic to enforce rules on sexual activity.

The use of vaccines to rid the world of disease was proven successful with smallpox. Smallpox was a devastating disease that killed thousands of people in its mildest sweeps across the world. Aggressive vaccination programs ensured that nobody in the world was infected with the virus by the end of the 1900s. As early as 1881, medical professionals were proposing the development of vaccines to wipe out syphilis. However, the project was abandoned because of the possibility of inducing syphilis from the vaccine. Vaccines produced up until the 1970s were usually made with weakened organisms. Sometimes the organisms were not weakened properly and managed to cause the disease they were meant to prevent. Today it is known that syphilis vaccines would not impart full immunity. The way *T. pallidum pallidum* enters and resides in the body prevents the immune system from completely countering an infection.

Figure 6.4 Education is a key element in controlling the spread of syphilis. Today, even young children are taught about the disease and how to prevent transmission. (© Monkey Business Images/shutterstock)

sis. There is always concern that *T. pallidum pallidum* could develop resistance to penicillin.

The incidence of syphilis worldwide remained unchanged from its first occurrence until the 1950s. It then dramatically declined after that period. Much of the reason for the decrease in syphilis immediately after 1950 was the advent of antibiotics. Syphilis was successfully curtailed, and in some cases eradicated, when antibiotics were administered to infected soldiers and prostitutes. However, this did not explain further declines in the disease. Public awareness played a big role after 1950. Government campaigns aimed at reducing STDs changed the philosophy of syphilis control from curing to preventing. Mandatory blood tests on soldiers guaranteed that they would not bring syphilis back home.

Many states began requiring syphilis tests for couples considering marriage. This caught many cases that would have gone undetected and reduced the transmission of the disease to spouses and children.

Churches, civic groups, and schools also contributed to the later decline of syphilis and other STDs. Children were continuously educated about abstinence and safe sex as methods for containing the spread of STDs. This included lessons on the proper selection and use of condoms. Some agencies started programs tailored for educating prostitutes about syphilis protection. Governments allowing legalized prostitution provided mandatory syphilis education and training tagged to a license for businesses conducting prostitution. This general public awareness of the disease helped people recognize syphilis. It also facilitated a better understanding of how it was contracted. Many of the successful programs were carried over to different nations through programs sponsored by the United Nations World Health Organization. Today, syphilis is not a mystery. It will continue to decline over the next decade as long as people remain aware of its potential to spread again in spite of accurate rapid diagnoses and effective treatments.

7

Syphilis in Contemporary Society

On October 29, 1878, a housekeeper was admitted to the London Royal Hospital for Diseases of the Chest. Her visit was prompted by severe throat swelling that was preventing her from swallowing and made it difficult to breathe. She told that physicians that she showed good health up until her marriage. Her parents were in good health and had no outstanding medical conditions. However, two years after the wedding she started to develop a vaginal discharge. Five years after that sores developed all over her body. The sores on her body disappeared, but were followed by sores on the tongue and throughout the mouth. Upon examination, the physicians discovered severe narrowing of the throat passageways that lead to the lungs and stomach. They eventually concluded by studying the sores in her mouth that she was afflicted with syphilis. The physicians had no successful means of treating her syphilis at such a late stage. All they could do was to surgically expand her throat to help her breathe and swallow.[1]

Knowledge about a disease teaches future generations valuable lessons for avoiding it. First-century Roman slave Publius Syrus summarizes this sentiment: "It is a good thing to learn caution by the misfortune of others."

Syphilis's first onslaught in Europe definitely brought calamity. People had little experience with diseases resembling syphilis. The closest epidemics they had encountered were anthrax, black plague, cholera, and smallpox. Syphilis, however, did not follow the same pattern of devastation presented by those diseases. Therefore, it was approached as a new situation involving all the trial-and-error learning strategies evident throughout recorded history. Because there was no universal interpretation of syphilis, people responded to the disease according to local beliefs.

Physicians in the 1500s handled syphilis as they would any other contagious disease. They limited their exposure to the patient to prevent their own deaths, a technique learned after several sweeps of black plague. The physicians also learned that treatment was ineffective and just aided further spread. Eventually, they discovered that syphilis was not as easily contagious as anthrax, black plague, cholera, and smallpox. Therefore, it was approached like leprosy, which the physicians understood required multiple close contacts for transmission of infection. Unfortunately, the similarity to leprosy reinforced the social stigma if syphilis. People with syphilis were tucked away in sanitariums to succumb to the disgusting disease—hidden from the eyes of the public. Hints of sexual transmission were becoming associated with syphilis, leading to a new line of thought that syphilis was a disease of illicit sexual activity.

In the 1600s through the 1700s, syphilis was seen as an ailment deserved by those afflicted. It did not spread to the "innocent." The disease was most prevalent in people who had promiscuous sex or visited prostitutes. Unfortunately, these negative attitudes prevented any organized efforts to specifically control and treat the disease. Syphilis became a moral lesson: Learn from those who have sinned to avoid the ravages of syphilis. Even the most well-respected public figures were denigrated to the ranks of people of weak character when the public discovered that they had contracted syphilis. Wealthy people were able to seek treatment for the symptoms—not to cure the disease but to alleviate the aches and pains. A growing concern for public health drove governments to find syphilis treatments, solely to limit the disease's unintentional distribution to all elements of society. Governments were afraid that people

SYPHILIS AND THE VIRGIN QUEEN

Queen Elizabeth I reined over England and Ireland from 1558 to 1603, during the height of the syphilis epidemic plaguing Europe. Elizabeth I was a daughter of Henry VIII, who was noted for many infamous acts during his reign. Her life was well chronicled with many facts and an equal number of myths. The two most noted events of her life were how she secured the throne and how she maintained the status of being a virgin. Her virginity was debated, especially because of rumors about her being afflicted with syphilis. Elizabeth I was not a shoe-in for the queen. Her mother's marriage to Henry VIII had been annulled, making Elizabeth an illegitimate successor to the throne. By luck there were no other natural heirs left to inherit the royalty. So she was the only person bearing Henry VIII's bloodline and was able to hold on to her tenuous position as queen.

Her status as a virgin was more difficult to assess. The queen publicly asserted her virginity, using it as a hallmark of her moral rectitude and righteousness. She also made it known to the British Parliament that she had no desire to produce an heir to the throne. Anecdotal evidence supports her claim of virginity. Her lack of privacy prevented any secret encounters leading to an affair. The idea that Elizabeth I had syphilis was probably a rumor meant to detract from her noble image. Her persistent stature as a virgin probably excluded her from contracting syphilis by sexual means. Claims that she acquired congenital syphilis from Henry VIII are unfounded because it was never proven that he or any of his wives had syphilis. No bone analysis was performed on the bodies to confirm the assertions of syphilis. Also, there are no records of the royal family having any physical signs of syphilis, although they displayed emotional and psychological symptoms that, at the time, were attributed to the disease.

who acquired the disease through lewd means would spread it to innocent spouses and ultimately to their children. This is why prostitutes in some countries were forced to be labeled, so people knew they were potential sources of disease.

Changing attitudes about sex fortuitously accompanied monumental discoveries in science and medicine. Just as *T. pallidum pallidum* was discovered, society was beginning to treat sex with less disdain. Medicine was allowed to cure the disease without criticism that it was perpetuating sin or contributing to the moral decline of society. Some small segments of American and European society protested developing cures for syphilis, refusing to abandon traditional beliefs. These people believed that medicine was interfering with the punishments meted out by God. Surprisingly, the concerns of these few traditionalists became evident in society. Antibiotic cures lulled people into the belief that infectious diseases were simply an inconvenience that could be eliminated with an injection or a pill. People, including many respected scientists and public health officials, saw antibiotics and vaccines as ways to completely eradicate disease. This confidence lifted many intense fears about the controllability of infectious disease outbreaks. It also erased many worries about beliefs and taboos believed to lead to disease. Could this attitude translate into the sentiment that sex would be less risky if syphilis were easily treatable or not a risk at all?

The initial introduction and unrelenting success of antibiotics, particularly the very effective penicillin G, brought joy to many people. However, it also aroused deep fears in just as many others. Some scientists felt that easy cures for syphilis would not discourage the improper attitudes leading to its propagation. Sometimes penicillin treatments were prohibited for certain "undesirable" members of society. This behavior appears prejudiced and callous today, but between the 1860s and 1940s some people considered it acceptable to allow **natural selection** to eliminate "weak" individuals from a population. A growing distaste for **eugenics** stifled this movement. Eugenics in humans is best described as the elimination of individuals having characteristics that, according to some people, genetically weaken humanity and could ultimately lead to human extinction. It was believed that letting such people die from an undesirable disease weeded "weaker" people from the human population.

Today, many people assume that science can create therapies for any human ailment. Every day, scientists find treatments for acutely fatal conditions such as leukemia and stroke. These past successes explain the frustrations of scientists and society over AIDS. People are astounded that science has not yet found a cure for AIDS. After all, more is known about AIDS than any other virus and the disease has been known for more than 20 years. Scientists are also frustrated. They cannot believe that they may never be able to discover a treatment that removes HIV from the body as well as penicillin G extracts *T. pallidum pallidum* from syphilitic bodies.

SYPHILIS IN THE FABRIC OF SOCIAL NORMS

STDs, unlike other infectious diseases, tell specific details about a person's life. In adults, such an infection screams out that one has had unprotected sex. Physicians know all too well the humiliation or anger they see when patients are told they have syphilis. The patients' feelings can be attributed both to the stigma of having syphilis and the fact that their personal lives have been exposed to a stranger. These negative emotions can also arise from the knowledge that the disease was given to them by an obviously unfaithful partner. Syphilis became interwoven with societal norms once it was identified as an STD. In the 1500s and 1600s, syphilis was thought to belittle particular cultures in which it was common because it was assumed that the disease accompanied vulgar sex. So emerged the terms "French Disease," "German Disease," and "Italian Disease." For those within a culture, syphilis was a sign of sexual intercourse with undesirable individuals such as foreigners, the depraved, and prostitutes. It was thought that a person diligently adhering to cultural norms would not have contracted this sexually transmitted disease.

The liberation of sexual attitudes and advent of serious treatments in the late 1800s and early 1900s changed the position of syphilis in society. The Victorian era was a time of increased freedom of art and emotion and at the same time it was prudish. Having syphilis became more of an indiscretion rather than an unforgivable character flaw. Syphilis was no longer seen as a eugenic punishment but as a slap on the wrist. This slap embarrassed some people, while becoming a badge of achievement for others. Visits to prostitutes were permissible as long as they were not flaunted or shared freely in daily conversation. Carrying the disease without seeking treatment was a forgivable weakness similar to consuming too much alcohol or smoking too many cigarettes. Public officials and high-profile people who contracted syphilis during this era were accused of folly rather than sin. This attitude changed as perceptions of sex changed.

A moral backlash hit America and Europe during the middle of the 1900s. Overt sexuality was not the norm anymore, especially for females. A rebirth of Freudian psychology set an ideology in motion that society must repress basic primitive instincts such as sexual enjoyment, including sexual activities such as masturbation. However, the onset of World War II put people in atypical situations that promoted sexuality. Soldiers left home pledging that they would remain sexually loyal to their current or future partners. Females were left with an unwanted and abrupt loss of intimacy as men disappeared into the war. Sex became a way to relieve stress for both men and women, and consequently there was a resurgence of syphilis. One important use of antibiotics during World War II was to minimize the rampant spread of syphilis. Soldiers were encouraged not to have sex. Military education programs taught soldiers how to avoid and recognize syphi-

Figure 7.1 The reign of Queen Victoria (1837–1901), pictured above, was a time of personal liberation and revolution. This resulted in sexual practices that promoted the spread of syphilis. (© Adoc-photos/Art Resource, NY)

lis. However, imprudence was forgiven and the soldiers were given treatment as if they had received a war casualty. Women at home were also treated. But these affairs were kept secret and subject to great admonishment if discovered. Syphilis temporarily tarnished a soldier's reputation but permanently destroyed the moral character of women. Among men, syphilis

Figure 7.2 The armed forces were very interested in controlling syphilis transmission among soldiers during and after World War II. Posters like this one were used to remind soldiers to think twice before having sex. (National Library of Medicine)

was a joke shared with buddies; for women it was a secret not even shared with one's closest friends.

A peak in sexual repression hit America just after World War II. Sex was not even acknowledged among couples with children. It was reserved for brazen and outcast people. Syphilis was once again viewed in a nefarious sense. Unlike in the previous decade, syphilis was again perceived to be the result of serious character flaws. Syphilis screening programs reached all sectors of society. Among the ranks of mandated syphilis testing candidates were prisoners, soldiers, and couples seeking marriage. A positive test for syphilis meant that a couple could not obtain a marriage license until the disease was treated and followed by subsequent negative tests. There was great concern that a positive test could result in the termination of the marriage plans.

Under the constraints of these attitudes, syphilis started becoming as much of a mystery disease as it had been in the 1500s. There was more of an emphasis on teaching abstinence than on promoting the values of safe sex. Syphilis education was primarily needed in high-risk situations such as in prison and military settings. These strict views of syphilis led to regulations requiring the reporting of syphilis cases to governmental agencies. The fear of being reported forced many people to seek alternative therapies, illegal care from unscrupulous physicians, or no treatment at all.

The 1950s ended with a dramatic swing in American sexual attitudes that the following decade was identified as the era of the sexual revolution. Sexual freedom was not just an acceptable ideology by the younger population most likely to be sexually active. It also became a prerequisite for fitting in with society. Syphilis became a sign of nonconformity with the repressive attitudes of the previous decade. It was also easily cured. Penicillin shots for syphilis were handled as nonchalantly as administering aspirin for headaches. Sex education shifted its focus from abstinence to safe sexual practices. The same types of condom use classes taught to soldiers during World War II were being used in high schools and colleges in the 1960s. Syphilis was no longer a stigma, and this new attitude permitted local governments to better track and document syphilis. People felt more willing to share information about

Figure 7.3 America withdrew into a period of sexual repression during the 1950s. Television and other forms of entertainment reflected this sexual conservatism. (© AP Images)

sexual partners, making it easier for the government to stop local outbreaks. This led to today's standard practice of questioning people about sexual partners after syphilis is diagnosed. This would not have been possible if the attitudes of the 1950s had prevailed.

Relaxed attitudes about sex followed the 1960s and remain part of contemporary American culture. Sex education, which in the 1950s was a topic best left at home and addressed only just before marriage, filtered down into the elementary education curriculum. At first, the safe sex information taught to children entering puberty was more of an attempt to ward off pregnancy than to reduce STDs. AIDS changed that attitude, however, and now STDs occupy a significant place in the instruction. Sex education has become such a commonplace theme in many schools that many children have little anticipation of the lessons and may at times ignore the information or put it in the same category as learning about math or grammar. Syphilis has taken on a role similar to that of the common cold. It is handled unemotionally as a preventable and curable disease. It does not carry the same badge of independence heralded in the 1960s. Rather, it is a sign that a person was careless or ignorant.

SYPHILIS IN RELATION TO OTHER STDs

Syphilis was the first known STD and has many more stories associated with it than the other diseases. However, the gradual eradication of syphilis has uncovered the other STDs described in Chapter 3. Gonorrhea was discovered during World War I but was not often recognized by the public until sex education became popular. This ignorance allowed it to perpetuate and remain as common as syphilis. By luck, it was restrained with the same precautions and treatments as syphilis, preventing it from becoming a modern plague. Gonorrhea did not get the same chance as syphilis to achieve universal notoriety. It was just another common STD. Similarly, chlamydial infection, chancroid, and the other bacterial STDs gain more interest among public health officials than among the average person. They are not a threat as long as they can be cured as simply as syphilis.

AIDS and genital herpes are not taken as lightly as syphilis. These viral diseases are proving to be incurable in spite of much effort using tremendous resources. AIDS has had much more impact on society because it is fatal and there was no treatment for a number of years. In the early days of treatment it even killed rapidly with aggressive therapeutic care. Any treatments that were developed only slowed down the progress of the disease or just relieved the signs and symptoms. The severity of AIDS conjured up attitudes that were almost identical to those about syphilis in the 1500s. Much blame has been directed at how this new uncontrollable plague began. First it was blamed on homosexuals and called the "gay cancer." This initial attitude exposed any ill feelings people had about homosexuals. As had occurred with syphilis, governments were battling over the origin of the first occurrence of AIDS. Most blamed the United States, while the United States was looking into evidence that the virus was imported from Europe by way of a gay male Canadian flight attendant. African nations were insulted over the research indicating that AIDS began there. Their argument is justified in light of the discovery of genes in European people that may provide protection from AIDS-like diseases. This means that disease may have originated in Europe.[2] Myths and erroneous stories still abound about steps that led up to AIDS becoming a human disease.

Syphilis made sex risky as soon as it was established as an STD. However, the concerns died down once antibiotics proved successful at fully curing the disease. AIDS refueled the idea that sex could have dangerous consequences. However, unlike syphilis, the lack of an immediate cure for AIDS is elevating societal concerns about the disease. The public is redefining its attitudes about sex, thanks again to the widespread occurrence of a stigmatic STD. Television shows and movies portraying casual and extramarital sex are gaining much criticism as a result of the spread of AIDS. Such entertainment is being accused of expanding unhealthy attitudes about sex and is being blamed for the high prevalence of unprotected sex. The rise in teen pregnancy and the reoccurrence of STDs are being used as evidence of the consequences of relaxed sexual attitudes. A further limitation to sexual freedom is the growing number of cases of multiple antibiotic-resistant bacterial STDs. This could raise syphilis to the status of AIDS if it once again proves to be an incurable disease due to antibiotic resistance.

8

A Case Study in Syphilis Research

In the late nineteenth and early twentieth centuries, scientists were interested in developing animal models to study a variety of human diseases. An investigation carried out in 1906 by Albert S. Grünbaum and Ralph D. Smedley at the University of Leeds in England looked at the feasibility of using chimpanzees to study syphilis. They replicated past attempts to introduce human diseases into apes. Grünbaum and Smedley carried out their experiment by introducing *Treponema* into the eyebrows of chimpanzees. They noticed some initial swelling and what at first seemed to be the progression of syphilis. Ultimately, the chimpanzees showed no signs of the spread of the bacterium and they remained in good general health. Studies in 1970 repeated the 1906 investigation to see if the chimpanzees' bodies had produced an immune response specifically against syphilis. They were successful at producing syphilis in the chimpanzees. However, it took a larger amount of bacteria to produce the disease than it would take in humans. They concluded that the chimpanzees would not be the best model to study human syphilis.[1]

Scientists learn about the nature of disease through extensive observations and precise experimental investigations. Eighteenth-century French writer Voltaire explained the characteristics of good medical research: "Nothing is more estimable than a physician who, having studied nature from his youth, knows the properties of the human body, the disease which assails it, the remedies which will benefit it, exercises his art with caution and pays equal attention to the rich and the poor." The

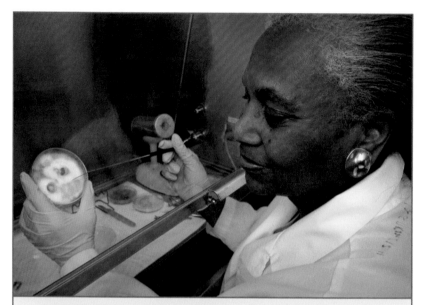

Figure 8.1 The scientific method allows for the consistency and accuracy of research. This scientist carefully inoculates bacteria on a plate to grow for further experiments. She must make sure that her results can be duplicated. (James Gathany/Centers for Disease Control and Prevention)

process, called the **scientific method**, ensures that any interpretations of nature made by scientists are as accurate and rational as possible. Over time, it provides an understanding of nature that is not biased by cultural differences, personal goals, or political motivations. Standard procedures such as Koch's Postulates are designed to promote consistency for particular types of investigations. Scientists claiming they know the cause of a disease using other methodology are justifiably scrutinized. Their findings are not acknowledged until similar conclusions are found using the accepted procedures. This initial reluctance to believe scientists using nonstandard techniques is not a form of snobbery but rather a way to protect the integrity of scientific information.

Two important assumptions are needed to follow the scientific method. First, scientists must assume that they are investigating measurable phenomena. Whatever they are studying must be detectable using universally accepted criteria and measurements. For example, a scientist investigating the cause of an infectious disease looks for a tangible life form, such as a microorganism, as the culprit. Viewing the organism under the microscope or detecting some characteristic chemical component can determine the presence or absence of a microorganism. Unique metabolic changes to the body can also be a clue to the organism's existence. These pieces of evidence can be documented and interpreted similarly by different people. Seeking a metaphysical or nonmeasurable disease agent, such as sin, provides no proof to substantiate the claim. There are no standard ways to measure sin. An alleged sinful act in one culture may be normal behavior in another. Sin is no longer considered a cause of diseases as it was before diseases were understood.

A second assumption of the scientific method is that experiments must show a relationship of cause and effect. When studying disease, this means that the scientist has to provide consistent evidence that the suspect organism is causing the disease. Isolating *T. pallidum pallidum* from a primary syphilis chancre or from the blood of an afflicted person does not prove that it causes the disease. This would be true even if every patient with syphilis had the same *T. pallidum pallidum* findings. All it means is that syphilis is accompanied by a *T. pallidum pallidum* infection.

Therefore, a researcher trying to prove that *T. pallidum pallidum* is the cause of syphilis must be able to introduce the disease into an organism with the intent of producing syphilis. Problems arise when diseases cannot be modeled in other organisms, as is the case with AIDS, where humans have to be the model. HIV only causes the AIDS disease in humans. Even chimps, which are genetically related to humans, do not

Figure 8.2 Walter Reed and his team of scientists researched the cause of yellow fever by experimenting on themselves. Some diseases, such as yellow fever, AIDS, and syphilis, can only be modeled in humans. (National Library of Medicine)

get AIDS. Walter Reed, a U.S. Army physician, came upon this problem when heading a commission studying yellow fever in Panama during the early 1900s. His dedicated team decided to infect themselves with the conjectured source of disease, sacrificing their health and the life of colleague Dr. Jesse Lazear when he died of the self-inflicted illness. Their altruism provided the information needed to control and prevent the debilitating and sometimes fatal disease.

The scientific method did not always address ethically correct ways to conduct experiments. Many scientists would agree that it is implicit in the scientific method that ethical practices must be used to collect data and formulate conclusions. Research studies involving humans are now subject to specific review and approval processes, ensuring that human subjects are treated ethically. Walter Reed's research borders the boundary between ethical and unethical. Some would argue that it was unethical to sacrifice his team to gain the knowledge they did. Others can counter by saying that their sacrifice was small compared to all the good it produced. However, what if Reed had tested his hypothesis on Panamanian villagers? Would his decision have had the same ethical foundation as his original choice?

Reed's decision to use his team as experimental subjects addresses the perception that the ultimate goal of science is the betterment of human society. Science contributes to society either by adding to a pool of knowledge that provides a better understanding of nature or by making life less precarious for people through the eradication of dangers and disease. However, inequities between countries and different segments of society prevent the rewards of science from benefiting all humans. The eighteenth-century philosopher Voltaire would find this somewhat disturbing; his humanitarian concerns for social equality led him to believe that all people should be respected and treated fairly.

Alexander Fleming's discovery of antibiotics was intended to help all of humanity. However, it only benefited those who could afford treatments and nations that had the money to fund research and produce **curative** drugs. Countries with the finances and technology to manufacture antibiotics gained great advantages by improving public health, thereby contributing to the further advancement of society. A country that has healthy citizens who can work and contribute to society translates into a better economy that permits innovations beyond what is needed for basic survival. Millions of people in developing nations do not have access to Fleming's 60-year-old discovery. This misfortune gives these nations little opportunity to progress equitably with countries that have regular access to curative therapies. This ethical issue is being addressed with diplomacy, foreign aid, and the establishment of agencies such as the United Nations World Health Organization.

During World War II, syphilis became a hallmark case study for evaluating and standardizing ethical practices in scientific research, particularly for research involving diseases that could only be studied on human subjects. A group of scientists crossed the boundaries of ethically acceptable research practices in an attempt to study the effectiveness of treating syphilis. The research question was important. However, the way it was conducted left many wondering about the value of the benefits achieved compared with the suffering caused by the study.

THE TUSKEGEE STUDY

An extraordinary speech made by President Clinton on May 16, 1997, put syphilis and research ethics together as top stories in the news. "Today all we can do is apologize but you have the power. Only you have the power to forgive. Your presence here shows us that you have shown a better path than your government did so long ago," commented President Clinton to the predominantly African American audience. Clinton's speech corresponded with the 60th anniversary of the Centers for Disease Control and Prevention (CDC). The CDC is a federal government agency tasked with the prevention, control, and monitoring of disease in the United States, as well as the promotion of good health through education and awareness

Figure 8.3 In 1997 President Clinton formally apologized to the surviving subjects of the Tuskegee Syphilis Experiment, 65 years after the unethical experiment began. Herman Shaw (right), a survivor, speaks at the ceremony. (© AFP/Getty Images)

initiatives. The people of whom he was asking forgiveness were survivors of the Tuskegee Syphilis Experiment. This infamous experiment used 600 underprivileged African American residents of Alabama for syphilis research. Herman Shaw, one of the experimental subjects, accepted the government's apology but followed up with the statement, "We were treated unfairly, to some extent like guinea pigs. The wounds that were inflicted upon us cannot be undone." What began as a government-sponsored investigation of syphilis ended up a catalyst for reforming ethics in human experimentation.

The Tuskegee Syphilis Experiment started out with an aspiration to better understand the progress of the then-incurable disease syphilis. In 1932, when the study was commissioned, syphilis treatments were only capable of remedying the signs and symptoms of the disease. Besides being ineffective, the standard treatments of bismuth and mercury, both highly toxic chemicals, sometimes caused more harm than the disease. Treatments usually led to kidney damage, liver failure, and neurologic conditions. Antibiotics had just been discovered in 1929 and were not yet in full use. It was not known until later that Fleming's penicillin would adequately rid the body of the disease. Most accounts of the natural history of syphilis were bits and pieces of anecdotal references from medical records. The traditional accounts from the 1700s and 1800s were inconsistent and seemed to be describing complications from diseases other than syphilis.

The U.S. Public Health Service searched for a way to study the progress of syphilis using a large number of human subjects. After all, the research of Metchnikoff and others showed that *T. pallidum pallidum* causes syphilis only in humans. The Public Health Service could have approached the study two ways: (1) infect a large group of volunteer human subjects with syphilis, or (2) find a large confined population of people already infected with the disease. This first option was undesirable but viable because the government could justify conducting the experiment on soldiers or prisoners. The second option would be difficult to carry out because a sizeable investigation would have to be done to find a population of subjects meeting the requirements of the study.

A chance economic development observation drove the Public Health Service to follow the second option for studying syphilis. In 1895, African American botanist Booker T. Washington called for a plan to improve economic gains for African Americans. He wanted an investigation into the factors keeping African Americans from gaining equal economic status with white Americans. A 1900 study conducted by the Tuskegee Institute showed that public health problems created issues hindering economic growth in African American populations. Accompanying this report were data about the incidence of syphilis among a poor African American community in Macon County, Alabama. It was found that 35 percent of the county's African American population had syphilis. An aggressive plan to reduce the incidence of syphilis in the community began with the Julius Rosenwald Fund. Factors related to the 1929 Wall Street Crash and subsequent Great Depression forced the Julius Rosenwald Fund to drop the syphilis program in 1931. This left a large proportion of Macon Country residents again without syphilis treatment.

It was instantly recognized that this now neglected population would be perfect for the Public Health Service study. So, in 1932, the Public Health Service worked together with the Tuskegee Institute to study the progress of syphilis in the Macon County residents. The project was called the Tuskegee Study of Untreated Syphilis in the Negro Male. It was agreed that no treatments could be given in order to study the scope of the disease from secondary syphilis through the tertiary stage. At the beginning of the study, before antibiotics, it was not clear that any available treatments actually improved outcomes. Subjects with primary syphilis were studied and then given standard treatments for the time. Apparently, there were enough subjects with progressive syphilis that it was viewed as unnecessary to withhold treatment from new syphilis cases. Syphilis was not intentionally inoculated into any of the subjects, contrary to what was claimed by many critics of the study. In addition, nobody was murdered to study the disease by autopsy. The experiment used 399 African American men diagnosed with syphilis and 201 without any indications of the disease. Subjects were unaware that they had syphilis and thought they were part of a study for a less severe ailment. Subjects were provided with free meals and medical care as long as long as they remained with the study. Data started flowing from as early as 1932 with investigators following the progression of the disease as it infected new individuals and progressed from primary to secondary syphilis in others.

Figure 8.4 Booker T. Washington (left) was born into slavery, but he procured an education and became a teacher. In 1881 he founded the Tuskegee Institute. Washington's dream of improving the plight of African Americans was deliberately twisted into a study exploiting them, when the institute was involved in a study that exploited hundreds of African Americans. (Library of Congress)

The study continued to produce useful data for the medical community well into World War II. Yet, by then it was established that penicillin was a suitable cure for syphilis.

Researchers hit a critical point of the study. They could end the investigation at that point by curing all the people with antibiotics, or they could continue their original research plan to withhold treatment until the study was completed. In 1945, the research team decided to withold antibiotic treatments from some subjects in spite of massive federally funded campaigns by the Public Health Service to eradicate syphilis in the United States. Again, subjects who developed primary syphilis during that time were treated with penicillin and subsequently dropped from the study. At first, the study was intended as a six-month project. However, the valuable information being collected permitted the investigators to extend the project. So, as syphilis waned in the United States, the Tuskegee study subjects were still suffering and dying from what had become an easily treatable disease, which many did not even know they had.

The study continued covertly until the late 1960s during the birth of the Civil Rights Movement. Public scrutiny of government agencies brought the Tuskegee study into the light. It was no longer a clandestine study but a cause to promote stricter ethical treatment of human subjects. A 1969 assessment by the CDC affirmed the need for the study as a necessary evil and supported the way it was being conducted. It was also backed by many physicians and by professional medical associations. This apparently did not satisfy civil rights groups. By 1970, the Tuskegee Study of Untreated Syphilis in the Negro Male was being disparaged in the press, which created strong public sentiment against the study. The publicity led the U.S. Congress to hold a hearing about terminating the project. In 1972, Congress agreed to end the study and provide antibiotic treatment for the remaining subjects. Unfortunately, penicillin does not undo the damage of secondary, latent, and tertiary syphilis. Amazingly, no formal apology was given to the subjects until President Clinton's 1997 address to the Tuskegee study survivors.

The Tuskegee University National Center for Bioethics in Research and Health Care was set up as a result of Clinton's speech, and a report was given to the CDC. The report was prepared by Dr. Vanessa Gamble, a physician and anthropologist at the University of Wisconsin. Her report identified the need for clear guidelines when doing medical research on human subjects. She included recommendations for training researchers who use federal money for research involving humans. This report convinced Clinton to establish the center for training researchers in bioethics. Two years after Clinton's promise, the Tuskegee University National Center for Bioethics in Research and Health Care was established in 1999.

THE FUTURE OF HUMAN EXPERIMENTATION

The Tuskegee study opened the door to inquiries into other human subject experiments carried out by various governments spanning 1880 through the 1970s. Eugenics programs carried out by the U.S. government from the 1920s through the 1950s were uncovered after persistent investigation by civil liberties groups. Forced sterilizations and medical maltreatment had been used in an attempt to eliminate "socially unacceptable" characteristics from the American population. Much of the research was paid for with government funds and conducted by premier research organizations such as Cold Spring Harbor Laboratory, the renowned genetics think tank in New York. Eugenics programs were banned after the 1950s as a result of public distaste for the strategies and new findings in inheritance research that exposed the naïve and incorrect assumptions of eugenics proponents.

Military scientists came under intense attack over many of the research studies carried out in their laboratories and medical hospitals. Especially during times of war, the individual rights of soldiers were waived for the benefit of national security. Many veterans of World War II were subjected to nuclear radiation experiments to study soldier performance during nuclear war. By 1953, it was becoming evident that military troops were purposely ordered to conduct maneuvers in areas having dangerous levels of radiation. The troops were then discreetly investigated for any health effects related to the radiation exposure. Radiation exposure was monitored with radiation badges, and the soldiers were not given any opportunities to discuss common illnesses that could be linked to contact with radiation. Field performance studies were also conducted. Sadly, any soldiers who left the military were not provided with medical follow-ups or treatment for illnesses related to radiation exposure. It is now known that many of the soldiers in these experiments developed cancers of the blood and major body organs.

Another set of military studies that gathered bad press was the army's drug testing program on lysergic acid diethylamide (LSD) and related experiments on biological and chemical warfare. The LSD studies took place between 1955 and 1958. Troops were given LSD to investigate its effects as a warfare-incapacitating agent. More than 1,000 soldiers were given the drug and evaluated for battle performance. The army was hoping to find ways of introducing LSD into enemy troops as a form of chemical warfare. The difficulties that would be involved in getting LSD into the rival troops caused military officials to seek a new direction for the research. They then conducted studies using LSD as a type of truth serum for interrogation. This line of research was also abandoned and the LSD studies were dropped. At least another 6,000 soldiers were believed to be involved in other chemical and biological warfare studies. Any documentation remains top secret. All accounts of the experiments are from the research subjects and retired military researchers involved in the projects. America is not alone in using soldiers as experimental subjects. A 2001 news story from Australia exposed similar experiments conducted by the British government.

Prisoners have also been used as supposed "volunteers" for human experimentation. Illinois Stateville Prison was the location of several research projects that took place during the 1940s. Hundreds of prisoners were infected with tropical diseases in attempts to study the diseases and find cures. Public awareness of the study coerced the governor of Illinois to form a medical ethics committee in 1947. The committee formulated strict guidelines for selecting and treating human research subjects. Many criticisms were made about using prison volunteers. Prisoners were coaxed into dangerous research studies by incentives such as reduced sentences and

THE TUSKEGEE LEGACY— AN AIDS CONSPIRACY THEORY

Medical experimentation on human volunteers is regularly conducted to gain information about new medications and treatments. These experiments, called clinical trials, are only conducted once a therapy has been proven safe on experimental animals. It is unethical and outright illegal to perform dangerous trials on humans. Government regulations and strict documentation guidelines must be followed when doing human research studies.

However, consideration for human well-being was not the situation in the Tuskegee Syphilis Experiment. The 399 African American males with advanced syphilis were given no information about the experiment in which they were the subjects. They were not volunteers, but rather unwilling participants whose dead bodies were autopsied to better understand the ravages of a prolonged syphilis infection. One physician involved in the experiment was quoted as saying, "We have no further interest in these patients until they die." Throughout the experiment, the men were led to believe that they were early parole. These enticements were heavily criticized because they forced prisoners into participating in activities for which they would normally not volunteer. In addition, it appalled the public when they learned that prisoners who would normally not have been released from prison were being let out on parole only because they participated in the research studies. A combination of public outrage and new views on civil liberties has halted human research studies on unsuspecting subjects and people susceptible to being coerced into volunteering. Syphilis, through the Tuskegee study, played a big role in defining medical research ethics in the twenty-first century.

getting medical care for the disease. It is known that at least 40 of the men spread the disease to their wives who then gave birth to a total of 19 children with congenital syphilis.

The inevitable discovery of the experiment by the media in 1972, of course, caused public outrage. People became very cautious about new medical treatments believing that they may be the unwitting subjects of an experiment. The African American community, in particular grew, very cautious of medical research and treatment. They were afraid of being victimized again because of racial prejudices. A 1990 survey indicated the long-term impact of the Tuskegee Syphilis Experiment on the African American community. It showed that 30 percent of the people involved suspected that AIDS may have been created by the government as an experimental organism designed to eliminate African Americans. This sentiment got international news coverage causing governmental agencies to publicly respond and discredit the allegation. Memories of the Tuskegee Syphilis Experiment contributed to the feelings of the survey respondents.

Ethical issues are still being raised by the Nazis' research on concentration camp prisoners carried out during World War II. Studies were done to determine medical practices for treating burns, drinking of seawater, freezing, high altitude sickness, and infected wounds. Other studies were done to show support for the Nazis' racist ideology or as a means of medically controlling the population of "undesirable" people. All of this research was conducted under inhumane conditions. Nazi records indicate that the prisoners were forced to be participate in the experiments and that almost all of the prisoners were subjected to extreme suffering. Many of the experiments were designed to eventually end the prisoner's life. In spite of the unethical methods, some scientists believe that it can yield valuable information that may help people today. Some of this Nazi medical data has been used in modern science for studies in which putting subjects in mortal danger would be unethical, but from which lifesaving treatments could be discovered. However, it remains an ethical and moral dilemma for researchers to draw any knowledge from data that came from such inhumane sources.

Currently, it can be very difficult to find people who are willing to be part of human medical experiments. These experiments are unlike those of the past. They are carried out in humane ways according to strict guidelines with clear informed consent procedures. They are usually reserved for testing new drugs to treat a variety of diseases. A current strategy for obtaining subjects is to contract research organizations in developing nations in Africa, Asia, Central America, and Mexico. These organizations pay people to be part of the experiments. In 2001, participants at the Conference on Ethical Aspects of Research in Developing Countries evaluated the implications of doing human research in these nations. They concluded that poor people in these countries are likely to take part in these studies solely to get money for their families. It was felt that the subjects would normally be unwilling to do so. However, the need for money led economically disadvantaged people to participate in a study even if it would cause harm. Most governments in North America and Europe have policies against coercing people into being research subjects.

SYPHILIS RESEARCH TODAY

Syphilis research today has advanced since the studies conducted in Tuskegee. Scientists now study syphilis animal models and in cells cultured in the laboratory. One recent animal study uses female and male Syrian hamsters to investigate congenital syphilis. The hamsters are injected with *T. pallidum endemicum*, which causes a disease similar to syphilis in rodents. Researchers can then monitor the success of the *Treponema* being passed from an infected male to an uninfected female or from an infected female to an uninfected male. They can also study how the *Treponema* is spread through an infected pregnant female to the fetuses and the young hamsters. Guinea pigs, mice, and rabbits were successfully used in recent studies using *T. pallidum*. These studies help investigators find ways to reduce the ability of the bacteria to spread from one animal to another. Medications or therapies can be tested that prevent the transmission. Chemotherapies have been tested on rabbits to treat drug-resistant *Treponema*.

Other studies involve cultivating *Treponema* in cells growing in laboratory containers. This permits researchers to study specific features of *Treponema* under conditions similar to the body. Animal or human cells are removed from the body and cultured in a sterile broth of chemicals that models body fluids. The cultures are then placed in an incubator that is kept warm and moist. These cells are provided with an atmosphere similar to what is found in the body. Cell culture incubators usually have an atmosphere of carbon dioxide, hydrogen, oxygen, and nitrogen gases. The levels of these gases model the fluids and tissues of the body.

Treponema bacteria are then placed in the cell cultures to watch how they live and respond to the cells. Researchers use cell culture studies to investigate how the bacteria stick to body cells in their attempt to penetrate tissues. They can also study how the bacteria damage particular cells and how the damage relates to signs and symptoms of syphilis. Scientists recently isolated chemicals from the body that encouraged the bacteria to adapt to different tissues of the body. This helps explain why the bacteria are able to spread readily to a variety of organs. Scientists were also able to study how particular cells of the body were able to combat the bacteria. These types of studies are too difficult to study in a whole organism.

Chemical and genetic studies are greatly advancing *Treponema* research. New types of testing allow scientists to better understand how the bacteria respond to the body and to various drugs without using animals or cells. One test, called microarrays, permits scientists to study how different genetic traits in the bacteria turn on and off as the bacteria carry out disease. Studies can also be conducted to see how the genetics of the infected organism respond to the *Treponema* bacteria. This helps researchers develop specific drugs that can control the genes of the bacteria or the infected person. Chemical and genetic studies also help scientists discover how syphilis is affected by other sexually transmitted diseases in a person. For example, it is now known why people with syphilis are more susceptible to AIDS. In addition, scientists have learned how to treat syphilis in AIDS patients.

Future directions in syphilis research are focusing on rapid ways of detecting *Treponema* from small body samples. This will permit medical doctors to discover patients just exposed to syphilis, helping them to treat the disease before it spreads further in the body. Early detection also reduces the transmission of syphilis to other people. Simple, low-cost syphilis testing is also being studied to help control syphilis in developing nations with high rates of syphilis. The low cost makes it more likely for poor countries to successfully implement the tests. Studies in Haiti, for example, are helping physicians identify syphilis in pregnant women in an attempt to reduce congenital syphilis.

Notes

Chapter 1

1. S. W. Parker, A. J. Stewart, M. N. Wren, et al., "Circumcision and Sexually Transmissible Disease," *Medical Journal of Australia* 2 (1983): 288–290.
2. Centers for Disease Control and Prevention, "Syphilis—CDC Fact Sheet," January 4, 2008, http://www.cdc.gov/std/syphilis/STDFact-Syphilis.htm#pregnant.

Chapter 2

1. M. Tholandi, A. Ellman, M. Samuel, G. Bolan, and J. Ruiz, "Estimation of Syphilis and Gonorrhea Co-morbidity Among AIDS cases in California," (National HIV Prevention Conference, Atlanta, Ga. July 27–30 2003).

Chapter 3

1. M. Tholandi et al, "Estimation of Syphilis and Gonorrhea Co-morbidity Among AIDS Cases in California," (National HIV Prevention Conference, Atlanta, July 27–30, 2003).

Chapter 4

1. M. Chaudhary, B. Kashyap, and P. Bhalla, "Congenital Syphilis, Still a Reality in 21st Century: A Case Report." *Journal of Medical Case Reports*, 1 (2007): 90.

Chapter 5

1. S. Rudavsky, "Lessons of Past Helping Curb Marion County Syphilis Outbreak: County Health Officials Report Positive Signs after Sharp Rise in Cases This Year." *Indianapolis Star*, August 25, 2008.

Chapter 6

1. A. Ronald, J. Kuypers, S. A. Lukehart, R. W. Peeling, and V. Pope, "Excellence in Sexually Transmitted Infection (STI) Diagnostics: Recognition of Past Successes and Strategies for the Future," *Sexually Transmitted Infections* 82 (2006): 47–52.

Chapter 7

1. T. G. Smith, and W. J. Walsham, "A Case of Extreme Pharyngeal Stenosis the Result of Syphilis," *Medico-Chirurgical Transactions* 63 (1880): 229–243.
2. S. M. Kaiser, H. S. Malik, and M. Emerman, "Restriction of an Extinct Retrovirus by the Human TRIM5a Protein," *Science* 316 (2007): 1756–1758.

Chapter 8

1. A. S. Grünbaum, and R. D. Smedley, "Note of the Transmissibility of Syphilis to Apes," *British Journal of Medicine* 1, 2359 (1906): 607; W. J. Brown, U. S. Kuhn, E. A.Tolliver, and L. C. Norins, "Experimental Syphilis in the Chimpanzee: Immunoglobulin Class of Early Antibodies Reactive with *Treponema Oallidum*," *British Journal of Venereal Diseases* 46, 3 (1970): 198–200.

acquired—A disease term meaning that a condition is picked up from a chemical, object, or organism.

AIDS—Abbreviation for *acquired immunodeficiency syndrome*. A sexually transmitted disease caused by the human immunodeficiency virus (HIV).

allergy—A condition in which the body produces an abnormally strong response to an environmental trigger or medication.

antibacterial—A medication that kills or prevents the spread of bacteria.

antibiotic—A drug used to kill or slow down the growth of bacteria.

antibiotic resistance—A condition in which bacteria are not harmed by antibiotics. May be caused by overuse of antibiotics.

antibody—A protein produced by the immune system used to fight disease.

antigen—A chemical on organisms that stimulates an immune response.

assay—A laboratory test used to detect chemicals or disease.

bacteria—A large group of simple microscopic organisms composed of one cell. Singular is bacterium.

bejel—Also called endemic syphilis, it is a contagious disease of tropical regions caused by a relative of syphilis called *Treponema pallidum endemicum.*

bloodletting—An old medical practice of draining blood and other fluids from the body to cure disease.

bubo—A swollen gland under the skin usually forming an inflamed lump. It is usually related to plague but sometimes confused with syphilis sores. Plural is buboes.

cadaver—A dead human body usually used for medical studies.

candida—A type of yeast that naturally lives on the skin and in the digestive system and reproductive tract of humans.

candidiasis—A disease caused by the yeast *Candida albicans.*

carbohydrate—One of the three main nutrients in food; found in starches and sugars.

Centers for Disease Control and Prevention (CDC)—A U.S. federal agency tasked with the prevention, control, and monitoring of disease, as well as the promotion of good health through education and awareness initiatives.

chancre—A hard sore or ulcer that forms at the point of contact with syphilis.

Glossary

chancroid—A contagious sexually transmitted disease caused by the bacterium *Haemophilus dycreyi*.

chlamydia—A common sexually transmitted disease caused by bacteria called *Chlamydia trachomatis*.

condom—A covering placed over the penis worn during sexual contact.

congenital—Acquired before or during birth.

contagious—A disease condition that can readily spread through a population.

curative—A treatment designed to permanently remove disease from the body.

diagnosis—A medical term describing the identification and naming of a disease in a person by recognizing the signs and symptoms.

disease—Any condition that causes illness or produces abnormal effects in the body.

ELISA—Abbreviation for *enzyme linked immunosorption assay*. A method for detecting small amounts of a chemical or disease organism.

epidemiological studies—Investigations into the cause and spread of disease.

epidemiology—A means of investigating the causes, transmission, and affected population of a disease.

eugenics—The selection of humans for desirable characteristics

fever—An abnormal rise in body temperature resulting from disease.

fibronectin—A mucous membrane protein to which many bacteria attach.

flocculation—The process of clumping together.

fluorescent—Giving off a glow under certain conditions.

FTA-ABS—Abbreviation for *fluorescent treponemal antibody absorption* test. A method for detecting syphilis.

fungi—A plantlike microscopic organism that feeds on decaying matter and living organisms.

genital herpes—A sexually transmitted disease caused by the herpesvirus.

genitals—The external or visible parts of the reproductive organs.

genital warts—A sexually transmitted disease caused by the human papillomavirus (HPV).

genitourinary—Relating to the organs of reproduction and liquid body waste removal.

gonorrhea—A sexually transmitted disease caused by the bacteria *Neisseria gonorrhea*.

gumma—A large soft lesion on the skin or internal organs.

hemagglutination—The clumping of red blood cells.

herbal remedies—Medical therapies using special plants or drugs extracted from these plants.

herpes—A contagious disease caused by the herpesvirus. One type is a sexually transmitted disease.

homeopathy—A philosophy of treating disease using very small amounts of drugs.

human immunodeficiency virus (HIV)—The virus that causes AIDS.

immune system—A complex system of body parts and cells that help recognize and fight off disease. Certain cells of the immune system produce antibodies.

immunoassay—A way of using antibodies to detect the presence of disease.

infection—Invasion of the body by a disease organism.

infectious—The ability of a disease to spread throughout the body and from one organism to another.

infertility—An inability to produce offspring.

inflammation—A reaction to injury involving pain, reddening, and swelling.

Jarisch-Herxheimer reaction—A severe fever caused by the use of some antibiotics.

latent syphilis—The stage following secondary syphilis. Patient shows no signs or symptoms of disease. The disease is spread throughout the body at this stage. It can last the lifetime of the infected person.

leeching—An old medical practice of using blood-sucking worms called leeches to drain blood from a patient.

lesion—An open sore on the skin or internal body parts.

microbe—Same as microorganism. A microscopic organism usually composed of one cell. Bacteria, fungi, protozoa, and viruses are microorganisms.

microorganism—Same as microbe. A microscopic organism usually composed of one cell. Bacteria, fungi, protozoa, and viruses are microorganisms.

monogamous—Having only one mate.

morbidity—Illness or disease attributed to an infectious agent or activity.

mucous membrane—A moist protective lining of the body that produces mucus. The digestive system, lungs, and reproductive tract are lined with mucus membranes.

mucus—A sticky fluid produced by mucous membranes.

natural selection—The survival of offspring that have favorable characteristics for living in a particular environment.

opportunistic—A condition when normal microorganism inhabitants of the body accidentally produce illness.

parasite—An organism that invades and feeds off another organism (the host), usually causing mild disease or harm. The parasite generally does not kill the host because it provides resources that the parasite needs to survive.

pathogen—An organism that causes disease.

pelvic inflammatory disease (PID)—An infection of the internal organs of the pelvis in females. It can be caused by untreated sexually transmitted diseases.

penicillin G—an antibiotic used to treat a variety of diseases caused by bacteria.

periodontal—Referring to the gums or the mouth.

pinta—A little-known contagious disease of tropical regions caused by a relative of syphilis called *Treponema carateum*.

polymerase chain reaction (PCR)—A chemical technique that uses small amounts of DNA to identify an organism.

primary syphilis—The first indication of syphilis. It is manifest by the appearance of a chancre. The stage can last from six weeks to several months. People are very contagious at this stage.

prostitute—A person who engages in prostitution.

prostitution—The performance of sexual acts for money.

protein—One of the three main nutrients in food needed for the body to function properly.

protozoa—Simple microscopic organisms composed of one cell. They are more complex than bacteria.

red blood cells—Blood cells that carry oxygen.

reproductive tract—All the external and internal parts of the body used in reproduction. It shares parts with the urinary system.

scientific method—The process by which scientists formulate an idea (a hypothesis), test that idea, and formulate new hypotheses from their results.

secondary syphilis—The stage following primary syphilis. At this stage, the organism spreads through the body causing sores and pain. It usually lasts three weeks to as long as a year.

sexually transmitted disease (STD)—An infectious disease spread by intimate contact and sexual activity.

sign—An indication of disease that can be measured or seen during diagnosis. Redness, sores, and swelling are examples of disease signs.

spirochete—A group of spiral-shaped bacteria that cause disease in a variety of organisms. Lyme disease and syphilis are caused by spirochetes.

symptom—An indication of disease that is subjectively experienced by the patient, but cannot be measured. Dizziness, headache, nausea, and pain are examples of disease symptoms.

syphilis—A sexually transmitted disease caused by the bacteria *Treponema pallidum pallidum*.

tertiary syphilis—The final stage of syphilis following the latent stage. It is recognized by fatal damage to many body organs including the brain.

therapy—A treatment for curing or lessening a disease.

TPHA—Abbreviation for *Treponema pallidum haemagglutination assay*. A method for detecting syphilis.

treponema—A group of spirochete bacteria known to cause disease in many organisms.

trichomoniasis—A sexually transmitted disease caused by the protozoan *Trichomonas vaginalis*.

urethritis—Irritation of the urethra. The urethra carries urine from the urinary bladder to outside the body.

urogenital—Relating to the organs of reproduction and liquid body waste removal.

vaginosis—A sexually transmitted disease causing irritation of vagina. It can be caused by a variety of microorganisms.

VDRL—Abbreviation for *Venereal Disease Research Laboratory*.

venereal—Pertaining to a sexually transmitted condition.

virus—A very small infectious agent that can only live within the cells of other organisms. It is generally composed of only genetic material and a protein coat.

yaws—A contagious skin disease of tropical regions caused by a relative of syphilis called *Treponema pallidum pertenue*.

Further Resources

Books and Articles

Andreski, Stanislav. *Syphilis, Puritanism and Witch Hunts: Historical Explanations in the Light of Medicine and Psychoanalysis with a Forecast about AIDS.* New York, Palgrave Macmillian: 1990.

Arrizabalaga, Jon. *The Great Pox: The French Disease in Renaissance Europe.* New Haven, CT, Yale University Press: 1997.

Brown, William Jordan. *Syphilis: A Synopsis.* Washington, D.C., U.S. Public Health Service: 2001.

Cefrey, Holly. *Syphilis and Other Sexually Transmitted Diseases.* New York, Rosen Publishing Group: 2002.

Diamond, Jared. *Guns, Germs, and Steel: The Fates of Human Societies.* New York, Norton: 1997.

Eatough, Geoffry. *Fracastoro's Syphilis: Introduction, Text, Translation and Notes.* Oakville, CT, David Brown Book Company: 1984.

Hayden, Deborah. *Pox: Genius, Madness, and the Mysteries of Syphilis.* New York, Basic Books.

Jones, James Howard. *Bad Blood: Tuskegee Syphilis Experiment.* New York, Free Press: 1993.

Larsen, Sandra, Victoria Pope, and Robert E. Johnson. *Syphilis: A Manual of Tests and Supplement.* 9th Edition. Washington, D.C., American Public Health Association: 1999.

Nester, Eugene, et al. *Microbiology: A Human Perspective*, 3rd Edition. New York, McGraw-Hill: 2001.

Poirier, Suzanne. *Chicago's War on Syphilis, 1937–1940: The Times, the Trib, and the Clap Doctor.* Urbana, University of Illinois Press: 1995.

Quetel, Claude, Brian Pike, and Judith Braddock. *History of Syphilis.* Baltimore, MD, Johns Hopkins University Press: 1999.

Reverby, Susan. *Tuskegee's Truths: Rethinking the Tuskegee Syphilis Study.* Chapel Hill, University of North Carolina Press: 2000.

Tilden, J.H. *Gonorrhea and Syphilis–1912: A Drugless Treatment of Venereal Diseases.* Kila, MT, Kessinger Publishing Company: 1998.

World Health Organization. *Handbook of Endemic Treponematoses: Yaws, Endemic Syphilis and Pinta.* New York, WHO Publications Centre: 2001.

Web Sites

The American Academy of Family Physicians
http://www.aafp.org

Centers for Disease Control and Prevention (CDC)
http://www.cdc.gov

eMedicineHealth
http://www.emedicinehealth.com

History of Syphilis
http://medinfo.ufl.edu/other/histmed/clancy

National Institute of Allergy and Infectious Diseases (National Institutes of Health)
http://www.niaid.nih.gov

National Library of Medicine: Medline Plus
http://www.nlm.nih.gov/medlineplus

Syphilis: Diagnosis and Management
http://www.stdservices.on.net/std/syphilis/management.htm

WebMd
http://www.webmd.com

About the Author

Dr. Brian Shmaefsky is a professor of biology and service learning coordinator at Lone Star College–Kingwood near Houston, Texas. He completed his undergraduate studies in biology at Brooklyn College in New York and completed his graduate studies at Southern Illinois University at Edwardsville and the University of Illinois. His research emphasis is in environmental physiology. Dr. Shmaefsky has many publications on science education, some appearing in *American Biology Teacher* and the *Journal of College Science Teaching*. He also has written books and technical articles on biotechnology and human diseases. Dr. Shmaefsky is also the author of a case studies anatomy and physiology textbooks. He is very active serving on local and international environmental awareness and policy committees. He has two children, Kathleen and Timothy, and lives in Kingwood, Texas, with his two dogs and a guinea pig.

About the Consulting Editor

Hilary Babcock, M.D., M.P.H., is an assistant professor of medicine at Washington University School of Medicine and Medical Director of Occupational Health for Barnes-Jewish Hospital and St. Louis Children's Hospital. She received her undergraduate degree from Brown University and her M.D. from the University of Texas Southwestern Medical Center at Dallas. After completing her residency, chief residency, and Infectious Disease fellowship at Barnes-Jewish Hospital, she joined the faculty of the Infectious Disease division. She completed an M.P.H. in Public Health from St. Louis University School of Public Health in 2006. She has lectured, taught, and written extensively about infectious diseases, their treatment, and their prevention. She is a member of numerous medical associations and is board certified in infectious disease. She lives in St. Louis, Missouri.